CELEBRATING THE SECOND YEAR OF LIFE

CELEBRATING THE SECOND YEAR OF LIFE:
A Parent's Guide for a Happy Child

Lucie W. Barber
and the Staff of the Union College
Character Research Project

Religious Education Press
Birmingham   Alabama

Library of Congress Cataloging in Publication Data

Barber, Lucie W
    Celebrating the second year of life.

    Bibliography: p. footnotes
    Includes index.
    1. Infants.   2.   Child development.   3.   Children—
Management.   I.   Union College, Schenectady.   Character
Research Project.   II.   Title.
HQ774.B33   649'.122   78-21484
ISBN 0-89135-015-2

Religious Education Press, Inc.
1531 Wellington Road
Birmingham, Alabama 35209
2   3   4   5   6   7   8   9   10

*Religious Education Press publishes books and educational materials exclusively
in religious education and in areas closely related to religious education. It is
committed to enhancing and professionalizing religious education through the
publication of significant scholarly and popular works.*

To
MY CHILDREN
TOM, MARNY, JEAN, ANNE, AND CATHY

CONTENTS

PREFACE

When I started writing this book, I had come to believe two things. First, that parents are the most effective teachers of little children. Second, that parenting skills of proven worth can help today's children have positive, constructive attitudes toward life. I am still convinced that these two things are, or readily can be, true.

I came to these beliefs with more than a little help. For the past ten years I have worked with Dr. Ernest M. Ligon at the Union College Character Research Project, where I was exposed to and deeply involved in research into the processes of attitude and value formation from infancy through adolescence. Since 1967, especially, my association with the Project's research curriculum for the parents of infants has been close and continuous. In addition, it was at the suggestion of a Project colleague, Herman Williams, that I began to focus my attention upon the specific details of development during the second year of life. My working context and the useful suggestions of my colleagues set the direction for this work, and I am grateful for that help. But I must be held accountable for all I have done with the data, for that is my responsibility.

Still, having said that, I am appreciative of the invaluable cooperation I have had from the entire staff of the Union College Character Research Project. I am particularly appreciative of the help I have had from Virginia Atherton, Helen Cernik, and Kimberly Barton of the research staff—and from Julia Bennett of our secretarial staff.

In addition, as this book was being written, I had the help of a number of readers outside the Project staff. I am particularly indebted to Mary Perkins Ryan, Sheila Moriarity O'Fahey, Thomas Wright, and Dr. C. R. Par-

tridge for their comments, critique, and support. I also
want to record my very special thanks to my husband, Dr.
John H. Peatling, for his professional advice and personal
support.

Now that this work has been completed, I find that I also
believe that the second year of life is a crucial period for
the development of a positive, healthy, and constructive
outlook upon life. I hope that the following pages will help
others to share this belief with me. In addition, I hope that
this belief will be held with joy, for the span between twelve
and twenty-four months should be celebrated. There can
be fun in parenting. While challenges abound, parents can
meet them and know the great satisfaction that comes
from competent, positive parenting.

Lucie W. Barber, Ed.D.
Director of Applied Research
Union College Character Research Project
Schenectady, New York

INTRODUCTION

Something is happening to parents. It's as though there is a brand new generation of them quite different from the Spock parents of the last two and half decades. The difference is not simple to explain. However, the end result is observable. More and more married couples in the 1970s consciously decide whether or not to become parents, and they make that deliberate choice child by child. These new parents are producing each child who is consciously and specifically wanted by the parents.

Back at the turn of the century the average number of children in a family was five! Society *expected* married couples to produce children. There were economic reasons. The farmer needed sons to help on the farm. The business man needed sons to take over the business. The wife's task was to raise the children and look after the house. Women became pregnant as the expected aftermath of marriage. Parents became parents without the clear choice being left up to them. The role of parent was thrust on people because of societal expectancies.

However, gradual and subtle changes have occurred since 1900 which are producing a new generation of parents in the 1970s. For example, the birth rate fell drastically during the Depression years for obvious economic reasons. The birthrate rose again after World War II during a period of prosperity. However, today, economic reasons again play a part in the lowering birthrate. The rate of inflation causes many couples to carefully consider if they can afford children at all and, if they can, how many children their income can accommodate.

The population explosion scare of the sixties caused many couples to reduce the number of children they planned to produce. By 1972 the average number of children per family was 2.3 and the rate continues to decline. Human ecology and a concern for the human environment becomes ever more prevalent and influential.

Human ecology and economic reasons are not the only forces for change. Consider what is happening to the role of women. They are becoming liberated from being, "just a housewife." Women are more and more choosing whether or not to become pregnant and even whether or not to continue a pregnancy. These choices are easier to make because of advances in medicine. Attitudes are changing and sex-role stereotyping is subsiding. Society no longer overwhelmingly expects women to produce babies and stay home with their children.

Changes in the wife's role have affected changes in the husband's role as well. Husbands can be liberated to be fathers in the best meaning of the term. In the process of drifting sex roles, many couples with working mothers find that fathers stay home and spend more time with their children. Many fathers are learning to enjoy their parenthood.

Humanism is another factor contributing to the change of societal expectancies influencing parents. More and more people of all ages have begun to inspect the meaning of being a human being. There must be more to humanness than competition and materialism. There is loving, creativity, and nurturing of the spirit. There is the worth of each individual person. Such concern for humanism has spread dramatically to potential parents. In this new generation of parents, each new child is wanted, planned for, and valued as a precious, individual, human being. This book is purposively directed to those parents who willingly intend to help their child become all that child is capable of becoming.

This new generation of parents, then, needs a new kind of baby book. You will still need the Spock and Ladies Home Journal baby books for making formulas, identifying rashes, and binding up wounds, because you will not find very much in this book about the physical well-being of your child. You will find an emphasis instead on the psychological well-being of your child. This book is about the very early attitude and value education of your child. It is written in the belief that the second year of a child's life is a crucial time for such education, and in the belief that parents are the ones to direct this education. The new generation of parents is already motivated in the direction of attitudes and values of human beings. This book will help them engage effectively in the attitude and value education of their own child.

Attitudes and values are caught. They can also be taught. They can be taught systematically and rationally by parents who are willing to become pararesearchers. This is good common sense. Effective parents research their child, whether they know it consciously or not, so that they can gear their training to their particular child. The home provides a unique climate for "individualized instruction" so difficult to attain in schools. You have the opportunity to research your child and become an effective teacher of attitudes and values. It is much more fun if you understand your child well and can "individualize" just for that child.

Too many people equate research with some cold, impersonal activity performed by scientists in sterile white laboratories. Perhaps that is true of physicists and chemists, who deal with impersonal protons, laser beams, and the like. But research in the social sciences deals with people and can be more personalized. Your research with your child will be warm and more personal because of your love and vision for your child.

The term "research" has been purposively chosen in order to draw your attention to your unique child. What is the research that parents can do? A well-known specialist in child development, Dr. Ira Gordon, puts it this way in introducing a book on games for parents to play with their very young children: "By careful observation, by trial and error, by seeing how your child responds and enjoys these games, you can decide how you will use them." It's as simple as that. You observe your child, you try something, then you analyze the results and revise, if necessary, recycling and repeating the procedure. That is the research you as parents are so well-suited to do. This book will show you how to rationally and with love engage in research so that your child's attitude and value education can be effective.

You will need knowledge of children in general. That is what you read about in all baby books. You will read about it in this book, too. However, that knowledge is not enough. You will need knowledge about your child in particular. You will gain that knowledge by observing your child, comparing your child to children in general, evaluating, and adapting. You will be shown how to evaluate systematically. You will be helped to organize information so that you can use it most effectively. But only you can do the actual research so that attitude education is accomplished with love and enjoyment.

Chapter 1

CHILDREN IN GENERAL

In order to begin your research for the attitude education of your child, you will need some knowledge of children in general. This knowledge will give you a place to start in the evaluation of your particular child and an understanding of what to expect in your child's development. To be sure, a general description of children in their second year of life will be only an approximation of your child. However, it will orient you to a study of your child from your child's point of view.

Parents often make the mistake of treating their young child like a miniature adult, a somewhat smaller edition of themselves, who thinks as they think (only in smaller amounts) and who perceives the world as they do (only from a lower level). This miniature adult idea needs to be corrected.[1] Parents need to realize two things about children and, especially, their own child: (a) a child's thinking and perceiving is vastly different from an adult's thinking and perceiving, and (b) your own child's thinking and perceiving is very different from yours.

You are now about to start your research by considering how children think and perceive. Such information will be found throughout this book, but we will begin by acquainting you with the work of the Swiss psychologist, Jean Piaget. Piaget has diligently observed the process of growth and development in very young children. The fol-

[1]The Swiss psychologist Jean Piaget calls this smaller edition idea "adultomorphism" in a book he wrote with Barbel Inhelder. See: Jean Piaget and Barbel Inhelder, *The Psychology of the Child* (New York: Basic Books, Inc., 1969), p. 21.

lowing set of selected notes are included for the benefit of those readers who are not yet acquainted with Piaget's important work. The period from birth to twelve months is included in order to place the all-important second year in perspective.[2]

Notes on the Work of Jean Piaget

At birth an infant is, in Piaget's view, "locked in egocentrism." This phrase means that infants are unaware of anything beyond themselves: they and their environment are indistinguishably one, and each is at the center of that whole. By the time a child is about two years of age, however, that child has moved through a series of successive stages which bridge the gap between being simply a biological organism to being also a social organism. This transition is quite an achievement.

Infants accomplish this transition by interacting with their environment and, as a result, adapting to it. Piaget calls this early period the sensory motor period, because it is through the five senses (i.e., seeing, feeling, hearing, smelling, and tasting) and as a result of motor activity that infants interact with their environment. At first, all the reactions of infants seem to be centered on themselves but, gradually, as they respond to stimuli coming from outside themselves, they begin to realize that they are *separate* from both the inanimate world around them and (even) the people who inhabit that world.

[2]The book, *If You Only Knew What Your Baby is Thinking,* Ligon, E., Barber, L., and Williams, H. (Burlingame, California: Panamedia, Inc. 1973), precedes this present book in that it covers birth to twelve months of age.

Piaget describes four stages within the sensory motor period which occur during the first year of life (0–12 months). The first stage (0–1 month) is one of complete egocentrism; the infant makes no distinction between self and nonself (or outer reality). Then, between one and four months of age, *chance* combinations of primitive reflexes form certain new response patterns in the infant. Next, between four and eight months, the infant repeats these new patterns with apparent intentionality. Finally, between eight and twelve months, more complex response patterns—both motor and perceptual—occur. During this fourth stage, anticipatory and intentional behavior emerges. For example, during this last stage a baby will push obstacles aside, or use a parent's hand as a means to achieve a desired end. Also, children are now beginning to realize that objects outside themselves are still there, even when they are hidden from sight. Piaget calls this important achievement "object constancy." Children at this stage realize that both objects and people have a permanent existence independent of that which they can actually see.

Now we come to the important second year of life (12–24 months). Children during this period are still developing and still moving further from extreme infant egocentrism. However, the path ahead is a long one. Children are still the center of their world, but they do begin to differentiate themselves from their environment. Their many explorations are their way of finding out about both themselves and their world. The world, at this stage of development, is markedly different from the world their parents see and know.

Between twelve and eighteen months of age, children engage in what can be called "directed groping." For example, they begin to experiment, in order to see what will happen. No longer do they simply repeat movements in order to produce a desired result. Instead, children now vary their movements to see how the results will differ. A common example of this experimentation is the child who drops bread crumbs from a high chair, in order to watch where each piece will land. Through trial and error, and often disorderly messes, a child learns new and differing means to achieve a desired goal. This learning is the beginning of recognizably intelligent behavior. The child is constantly learning by interacting with the environment.

The period of "directed groping" from twelve to eighteen months of age can be divided into two halves, because at around fifteen months an interesting conflict reaches a peak. As a young child perfects walking, running, and climbing skills, self-assertiveness and independence increases. However, during this same period of months a child has begun to communicate verbally. But it is usually just a beginning upon the complex task of talking. The imperfect talking abilities of a child often become a source of personal frustration because, although independence in moving about progresses, the child is, thus far, *not* verbally independent. This struggle to become initially and basically independent in language as well as in motor skills is nowhere nearly as frustrating to the child in the period of twelve to fifteen months of age as it is in the succeeding period of fifteen to eighteen months.

The last stage of sensory motor period behavior, occurs roughly between eighteen and twenty-four months of age and represents still further developmental progress for most children. A child during this period begins "groping" mentally, rather than physically. The child *thinks* about how to do something, without actually having to do it. The "groping" physically still goes on, but now the mental activity is added. As this happens, a child is making a transition from physical operations to mental operations. That is a major step.

In summary, all of the accomplishments during the first twenty-four months of life add to children's awareness of themselves as persons separate from other people. Most children accomplish five vital tasks by the age of two, or thereabouts. They achieve object constancy. They develop a primitive notion of causality. They acquire a rudimentary concept of space and an equally rudimentary concept of time (for example they can locate their toys, and know that daily events have a certain sequence). They begin to retain mental images somewhat beyond their immediate sensory experience. They can anticipate coming events. These five accomplishments are fundamental to all further development.

Children at two years of age, however, still have a long way to go to become the truly social, intelligent humans their parents hope they will become. For instance, at two years of age children really do not care what effect their actions have on others, except as their actions bring them either pleasure or pain. They are still, in this way, quite egocentric.

The reader can understand now why a theme running throughout this book is *awareness*. We will be speaking about children's awareness of themselves, awareness of the environment about them, and awareness of people. You will also understand from the notes on Piaget why we will use the age categories of twelve to fifteen months, fifteen to eighteen months, and eighteen to twenty-four months. Children generally can be categorized this way because of their level of development. This does not mean that any particular child can be categorized because of age. This will be discussed again when we start considering your particular child. However, there is another important area that will help you understand children in general.

Learning How Children Learn

A young child in the second year of life is *not* a miniature adult. Therefore, learning is not the kind readily understood by adults. Again, Piaget's work is of particular interest because so much of what he has to say involves cognition. Learning requires cognition in the traditional sense. In order to learn the three R's (reading, writing, and arithmetic), mental operations (cognitions) are involved. However, Piagetian theory is broader, more all-encompassing. His theory generalizes to combine the biologically produced brain with the culturally produced environment. The infant learns by interacting with the environment. These interactions lead to adaptations which, sufficient or nonsufficient, determine cognitive structures. In other words, what the very young child learns is a product of interaction with the environment.

The idea of interaction emphasizes the necessity of stressing not only the child, a biological being, but also the environment. Of course, parents provide their child with an environment. The learning the child achieves depends upon both the child's genetic inheritance and the environment provided by parents.

Consider one child, Gale, as an example. Gale achieved a standing position at eleven months. She had developed sufficiently to allow this behavior to occur. Her parents were aware of the development of children, in general, thus they predicted that their child's first steps would soon follow. These first steps probably would occur naturally. However, learning to walk is the result of a child interacting with the environment and Gale's parents could have regulated an environment in such a way that she could not walk. Most parents, however, take great pride in their child's first steps. They arrange the environment so that their child has maximum opportunity. Gale's parents studied their child's progress so that they did not push too fast or impede Gale when she was ready to take that first step.

Now, because Gale's parents genuinely loved their child and wanted the very best for her, the third essential element to her learning was added. Once parents know children in general and their child in particular, they can add to their knowledge what they will also learn from this book—ways to help their child experience and build those basic outlooks which will determine their child's future values and attitudes. When a child acts—in this case, Gale's taking those first few steps—the action brings her into a further interaction with the environment. The environment, so to speak, "feeds back" something to the child. She learns "when I do thus and such, this results." The "experiencing" of such feedback is the real "stuff" of learning. It is upon that experiencing that cognitive structures expand and develop.

Did Gale experience the warm response of love and encouragement, or the response of inhibition and restriction?

Were her first steps greeted with praise or were they ignored or, even, punished by hostile parents?

Gale's parents fortunately understood their part in arranging the environment so that their child's first steps could occur. They also understood the crucial importance of the feedback they provide. They saw the opportunity to help Gale lay some groundwork for positive attitudes. While Gail learned to walk, she also received an early lesson on such preattitudinal goals as perceiving "the joy of exploring and learning" and "that achievement is satisfying." Gale's parents made certain that the feedback was fun and joyful. They saw to it that their child's first steps were satisfying. They lovingly gave their attention, their praise, and their encouragement.

Knowledge of children in general, knowledge of the unique child in particular, and knowledge of the importance of feedback in helping the child lay the groundwork for positive, basic outlooks have been stressed. More needs to be said about feedback because here is a cycling back to the first two types of knowledge again: What kind of feedback "works" for children in general and, more important, what "works" for your unique child? This book can tell you what is effective, desirable feedback for children in general. At least, this book can show you what happens with lots of different children. However, no book can tell you what will work with your particular child. That will be your joy to find out for yourself.

This book will give you suggestions, but you can be the researcher of your own child. You will have to choose from the suggestions that are given. You can try them and then evaluate their effect and continually adapt them to your child. Remember, your child receives feedback, one way or another, good or bad, desirable or undesirable. However, with a bit of study you, the parent, can organize and plan that feedback to best benefit your child.

We have tried to emphasize that your parenting can be fun and loving. The task will become easier and easier as you go along. There is one more point to emphasize: by training your child *now* toward positive attitudes, you will be saving yourself and your child a great deal of trouble later on. Some parents raise tyrants because they are too permissive. Other parents raise resentful, angry children because they are too authoritarian. In this book you will find a new approach to positive parenting.

Chapter 2

WHAT CAN YOUR CHILD LEARN?

The reader has considered children in general and *how* they learn. Now let us consider *what* they learn. Since value and attitude education is the purpose of this book and the reason for your research of your child, what attitudes can be learned?

It is good to be cautious when talking about forming attitudes in children so very young. It is probably more accurate to talk about laying a groundwork, or building a foundation for what with time will become recognizable attitudes. For it is only somewhat later, as a child matures, that what adults think of as attitudes are actually found in children. In this second year of life, however, certain basic outlooks that may have already begun in the first year do begin to develop and become entrenched.

These basic outlooks are largely the result of the child's experiences of living. In this book, five basic outlooks are identified. These five basic outlooks can be described in terms of five possibilities open to a child between the first and second birthdays:

1. A child can experience the joy of learning by exploring.
2. A child can begin to develop self-confidence and independence.
3. A child can begin to recognize selfhood.
4. A child can begin to associate happily with other people.
5. A child can learn that the environment is predictable.

These five possibilities can become accomplishments

during the second year of life. When that happens, these accomplishments form the foundations for a healthy and a happy personality in the future. However, unless parents (or someone) help a child during this important second year, a child's development of basically positive attitudes will be either retarded or crippled. But that need not happen.

From the moment of birth, a child is always learning *something*. If a child's experiences are negative, then future attitudes are all too likely to be negative. For example, a baby's explorations of the environment that are met with slapped hands or parental disapproval effectively teach that child that exploration is not any fun. In much the same way, if feeding and dressing are always administered by adults, a child learns to remain dependent. Also, if a child's daily routines and family schedule are constantly changing—if family life is in turmoil—a child learns to be insecure and untrusting. You will be able to help your child have positive experiences and build toward positive basic outlooks by "using," as it were, your baby's growing awareness of self, environment, and people.

How to Proceed

In the second appendix of this book you will find a chart for each area of awareness. These charts will be your bridge to the heart of this book in chapter 3. Rather than keeping you from starting with your child right away, you are being directed to these charts. However, many of you will have questions as you study the charts. For example, where are the basic outlooks? How do the columns relate to each other? You will find that information in the appendix when and if you desire to read about the complexities upon which the charts were built. However, you can use the charts without additional explanation.

The charts will provide information about children in general, your child in particular, and a step toward a basic outlook which your child can learn. Finally, the charts will give you the page number in chapter 3 where teaching suggestions will be found for steps you choose to take with your child toward basic outlooks.

The charts are not meant to cover everything children can do. The "abilities" listed are highlights of developing children. There are three charts and they are interrelated. In other words, a specific ability listed under awareness of self may be related to several basic outlooks. The appendix explains this interrelationship. The charts are just an easy way of organizing complexities. And your child is complex. Your challenge is to use the charts and chapter 3 in the flexible way best suited to your child.

One last comment about the charts. Don't make the mistake of comparing your child to anyone else's. The age levels are only very general guides. Every child develops at a particular rate of speed. The purpose of the charts is to help you identify where *your* child is developmentally, and the chapter 3 suggestions are your aid in moving a step at a time according to your child's rate of speed along the steps which lead toward positive basic outlooks.

Instructions for the Use of the Charts

STEP ONE: Read down the column "Specific Abilities of Children in General."
             Children's abilities become more and more

complex as they are increasingly aware of their selves, their environment, and the people around them.

As you read down the list of abilities, try to sense this developmental sequence.

STEP TWO: Now read down the list of specific abilities with your child in mind; what can your son or daughter do now?

STEP THREE: Place a check mark in the empty box to the right of each specific ability that your child has already thoroughly mastered. (You may want to date your check marks because you probably will use each chart again in a few months to assess further development of your child).

You now have a rough estimate of the present developmental level of your child.

You also have an idea of the next developments that are probable for your child.

STEP FOUR: Choose a specific ability your child has not yet fully mastered. Look opposite this ability to the next column to find out what step you can take with your child in teaching basic outlooks.

STEP FIVE: Once you have decided upon a specific ability and a step, look in the next column for the page number in chapter 3 for suggestions on how to proceed.

If you are using this chart for the first time, you will benefit by reading the introduction to chapter 3. General guiding principles will be found there that apply to all the sections in that chapter.

SUGGESTIONS FOR YOUR CHILD'S PROGRESS

Introduction

There are fifty-four sections in this chapter, one section for each of the specific abilities described on the charts in Appendix II. Each section provides three kinds of information. First, the specific ability will be discussed in terms of its importance to the developing child. A behavior that may seem inconsequential to you can have vast importance to your child. Here is where you will find the reasons that these particular abilities are important to your child.

The other two kinds of information have to do with how you can arrange your child's environment in order to research your child. You will receive suggestions for arranging the environment so that your child has ample opportunity for practice. And finally, you will receive suggestions about the environment that is you. You will recall that basic outlooks are learned as your child interacts with the environment and receives feedback from the environment. It is the feedback from you, how you respond to your child's actions, that you can experiment with in order to teach positive basic outlooks. You will receive suggestions that have worked for other parents. Adapt them to your child, try them out, and evaluate your success or lack of success. Repeat the cycle until your observations help you to be a skillful, loving parent in the attitude education of your child.

Before actually beginning the fifty-four sections, there are five guiding principles you can follow which apply equally to all fifty-four sections. It will be worth your while to consider them and use them, because they will help you in this new approach to positive parenting.

You Must Be Positive

This first principle hardly needs to be said because you are almost certainly aware of it. If you want to teach positive attitudes, *you* must be positive. But being positive is not as simple as it appears. When you survey a kitchen floor that your child has smeared with mud, or a tablecloth decorated with spinach puree, or an overflowing bathtub, you will have difficulty in maintaining your positive outlook. There will be times when the situation is too much for you, and you will lose your temper. You will need to make a yeoman effort to remember your child's perception of the situation. You can't expect your child to place the same priority you do on a shining floor, a clean tablecloth, or avoiding leaks through the ceiling. In the small world a child perceives, your child was exploring new forms of decorating. Mud, puree, and water are new media just discovered. If you scold or punish, as you will be sorely tempted to do, you run the risk of retarding your child's development of positive outlooks.

This may sound terribly permissive, and that misinterpretation must be corrected. Of course, your child cannot be allowed to forever track in mud, mess up tablecloths, or let the bath water overflow. Your patient guidance is needed in order to overcome these so-called delinquencies. Even though your child cannot appreciate what may be, from your perspective, misdeeds, you can gradually correct behavior. But you can do this without jeopardizing your child's attainment of positive basic outlooks. Your parenting skills depend on your remaining positive. Perhaps you can play a game with yourself. The rules are simple. Always look for the positive in every situation and respond *first* to that. Of course, along the way, you've got to guide your child in mud, puree, and water control, but you can accomplish this with greater ease if you first support your child's explorations and discoveries. In this way you demonstrate that you respect your child as a person. With the establishment of mutual respect and trust, it will be much easier, and more effective in the long run, to get your adult rules across.

Keep Life Fun

A second general principle is simply to keep life fun. Your child will respond much more eagerly if a learning situation is richly saturated with good humor, laughing, and play. Whenever you can, make a game of whatever you are trying to teach your child. This leads to a third general principle.

No Sermons

The very young child simply cannot use lengthy explanations or detailed reasoning, no matter how good an orator you are. One game is worth any number of sermons. Allow for action and keep it fun. Do not lecture.

Reward Positive Behavior

The fourth general principle has to do with rewarding desired behavior. Reward only desired behavior; do not reward undesired behavior. When your child plays quietly while you are on the phone, give a reward of a special hug or a treasured toy. Is this bribery? Of course it is, if you care to look at it that way. However, it works. It is based on conditioned learning principles. If B. F. Skinner makes you uneasy, consider this: your child is learning all the time whether or not you take part in conditioning. Your son or daughter will receive rewards from the environment, from other people, or from pleasureable feelings when objects feel, taste, or smell good. Wouldn't you rather join what is occurring anyway, and have a say in what "shapes" your child?

Do not reward undesired behavior. This part of shaping, called "extinction," is not so easy in practice. Children will cry when they do not get their own way. If parents plead with them to dry their tears, just this attention may be rewarding to them. Parents are then reinforcing the crying behavior. When you have determined that your child's crying is no more than attention-seeking or anger, be careful not to reward in any way. Ignore the tears, divert attention, and get your child started on another activity. Then give a reward for the new behavior.

Rewards come in all sorts and sizes. What is rewarding to one child is not necessarily rewarding to another. Cuddling rewards some, while other children will squirm and wiggle to be free of an embrace. Just your approving smile may be ample reward. Rewards also can be physical objects. A picture card for hanging up a coat may work. You can try cookies, stars on charts, magic badges, and so forth. You will find out what rewards your unique child as you carry on your research.

In case some readers feel squeamish about material rewards, fearing that their child will always demand such prizes, let us make the distinction between extrinsic and intrinsic motivation. Certainly, material rewards are extrinsic motivators and eventually you will want your child's motivation to come from within (intrinsic). However, when you consider developmental sequences of awareness, you realize that most very early motivators must be extrinsic, from outside the child. It is only as the child becomes more and more aware of self, environment, and other people, that behavior is motivated solely on an intrinsic level. The very young child is motivated by feelings that bring pleasure. Material rewards generally bring self-pleasure. Do not be afraid to use what works. That is your starting point.

As your child grows in awareness and forms the positive basic outlooks we have been talking about, material rewards will cease to be expected because their value will decrease. The intrinsic pleasure of learning and relating to other people will become a much more satisfying motivation.

Keep Records

Perhaps you can remember what works and what does not work with your child as you carry on your research. Most of us cannot remember; we keep records. You might buy a notebook and divide it into three sections, one for each of the areas of awareness (self, environment, and people). Then, within sections you can label a page for the specific ability you have chosen. Here is a sample of a record page which might be a helpful model for you:

AWARENESS OF————

A STEP CHILDREN CAN TAKE

SPECIFIC ABILITY NO.——

_____
_____
_____

_____
_____
_____

_____

_____

DATE   HERE IS WHAT I TRIED   HERE IS WHAT HAPPENED

Treasure this second year of life as your golden opportunity to help lay the groundwork for the rest of your child's life. This is a year when because of your child's growing awareness you are the most important part of the environment. You can express your gratitude for the gift of this precious year by helping your child build positive basic outlooks for the future.

Awareness of Self
12–15 months

A STEP CHILDREN CAN TAKE
To learn that achievement
is satisfying

SPECIFIC ABILITY NO. 1
They can pull themselves
to a standing position

1. What this ability means to children

Most children can pull themselves to a standing position by their first birthday. However, some may take longer. After all, a great deal of maturation must precede this momentous event. Some researchers have identified sixteen separate stages of development that must precede standing.

Watch your child struggle and pull up. In their determination children are likely to forget that once up they do not know how to get down again. They may howl in a frenzy, finally let go of their support and crash to a landing in amazement. However, they will try again and again to pull themselves up because it is new and exciting. They are learning to make their bodies do what they want them to do. And they are doing it by themselves without having to depend on their parents. What an opportunity to learn about the satisfaction of achievement!

2. Parents can provide

You will want to seize this opportunity because this stage does not last long. Probably in another month or sooner your child will be walking. Now, the achievement is pulling up to a standing position. Thus, your first task is to make sure there are supports available to your child to grab hold of. The most common, of course, is the playpen rail. This is a good place for your child to practice because the pad makes the crash landings somewhat less damaging than a bare floor. However, playpens or, at least, cooping the child up in them is frowned upon as inhibiting crawling. Another common support is parents' hands or legs. Your child probably will try tables, chairs, anything handy. Be alert to supports that are unstable, so that accidents can be prevented. Remove that wobbly end table.

3. Feedback

Your child undoubtedly will be pleased with the success of finally pulling up to a standing position. You can add to this satisfaction by the way you react to the new achievement. Praise the success with a hug, a cheer, maybe a kiss. You don't have to overdo it, but show your child that you appreciate the new achievement. Restrain yourself from over-concern with falls, lest by your attention you unintentionally reinforce the falling behavior. Unless your child is really hurt, ignore the inevitable falls. But reward the successes so that your child's achievement is satisfying. This will be an early lesson in learning self-confidence and independence. It will build toward your child's eventually discovering selfhood which began at birth, of course, but develops more quickly now as awareness of self increases.

Awareness of Self
12–15 Months

A STEP CHILDREN CAN TAKE
To learn that achievement
is satisfying

SPECIFIC ABILITY NO. 2
They can stand alone

1. What this ability means to children

Can you imagine how daring it must be for a child to stand unaided for the very first time? Suddenly the child becomes a two-legged human being. The stance may be strange looking, at least for a while; feet far apart, the toes turned out, knees locked, and head and trunk slightly forward. Your child stands like this to maintain balance, which isn't easy for someone standing alone for the first time. Falls will be frequent and are generally backward. But what an achievement standing alone must be! Your child is getting up in the world. Things will look different and there is more to see. Most important, though, is that the child has attained this lofty position independently. Your accolade for this achievement is well deserved.

2. Parents can provide

See to it that your child has ample opportunity to practice getting up into a standing position. You can hold a favorite object above your child to encourage standing and reaching for it. Together you can play "get up, sit down" games. Have your child stand by the screen door or a window to watch for members of the family coming home. You can point out the new things to be seen in a standing position.

3. Feedback

Above all, show your child how pleased you are with this new achievement. Reward success with praise. Overlook falls unless, of course, real hurts occur. The feedback you give determines what your child learns from this new experience of standing. If you react with pleasure, your child will learn that achievement is a satisfying experience. These experiences will add to your child's self-confidence and eventual independence.

Awareness of Self
12–15 Months

A STEP CHILDREN CAN TAKE
To learn that there is joy
in exploring on their own

SPECIFIC ABILITY NO. 3
They can walk

1. What this ability means to children

The length of time between first standing alone and first taking a step differs for different children. It usually varies from one day to one month. However, the great day will come, perhaps when you least expect it. A child may cruise for days holding on to things, then suddenly decide to let go and cross an open space all alone. Really those first steps are pretty comical. The child's arms may reach out to maintain balance or they may be held up close to the body. Eyes look forward rather than down, again to maintain balance. Thus, a lot of tripping and walking into objects can be expected. Falls will be frequent for most early walkers.

Do you realize what it means to children to learn how to walk? For one thing, it means they can get to more places and get there faster. Children find this new skill fascinating and will practice and practice. Some children, in their determination to walk, seem to forget all about learning to talk. It's as though walking and talking are both so important that children can only take on one or the other skill at a time. Walking is also important to children because they now have a new tool to use to satisfy their curiosity. The child becomes a highly mobile explorer. Of course, walking introduces a new set of problems for parents. You do have to protect your young Columbus from danger. You'll want to protect your house, too!

A little common sense and your positive attitude are going to help. Put gates across stairways. Remove breakable objects where your child will be walking. Put door latches or locks where your child cannot reach them. With security measures taken care of, remember, you want your child to learn that there is joy in exploring independently. That means that *you* must be joyous about your child's exploring. This attitude of yours takes precedence over your distress when your child receives minor bumps and bruises. It takes precedence over your anguish when breakage occurs around the house. It is more important, in the long run, for your child to learn about the joy of exploring. This is an important step toward your child's future self-confidence and independence.

2. Parents can provide

During the first two weeks or so of walking, just the fact of walking must be explored by the child. Most children increase their amount of walking by leaps and bounds after that initial period of tentativeness. Provide frequent opportunities for your child to walk. Lay out courses to be walked, with a treasure at the end. Gradually increase the length of these courses. When you are outdoors with the stroller, let your child get out and walk independently until tired. Praise and enjoy these precious days as your child explores the ability to walk.

Soon your child will use the ability to walk to explore the surroundings. Try not to limit these explorations any more than is essential for safety reasons. Of course, explorations across busy streets are not allowed, but there is nothing wrong with explorations around rooms in a house, or explorations all over the yard, or explorations in the park. Naturally, you will have to keep a close eye on your child, but freedom to explore is important so that the joy of explorations is learned.

Play some games with your child. A favorite for many is the "where is" game. Ask your child, "Where is the kitchen," or "Where is the clothes hamper," etc., and let the child walk there. Variations of hide-and-seek are fun.

Hide yourself or an object and call your child to explore until the object is found. Let your child have a turn doing the hiding, too.

Encourage exploration outdoors, too. Think of all the things your child can find walking about. "Find me a leaf" (or big tree, or a branch, etc.). Let your child walk to the object and touch it or point to it.

Children often will make up games of their own as they find that exploring is fun. The games may seem overly simple to you. However, that makes little difference as long as your child is using the ability to walk to experience the joy of exploring.

3. Feedback

Remember to praise your child for exploring, particularly when explorations are done independently. As your child receives praise and experiences joy, important groundwork for all future learning by exploring will be laid.

Awareness of Self
12–15 Months

A STEP CHILDREN CAN TAKE
To learn that there is joy
in exploring on their own

SPECIFIC ABILITY NO. 4
They can climb

1. What this ability means to children

The ability to climb may develop gradually or may seem to happen overnight. Some children love to get under chairs and climb over and under chair rungs. Some children climb up on the couch, up the back of the couch and onto a book shelf. You may discover your child perched on an end table or in the middle of your dinner table. Climbing stairs is another favorite of small explorers. All this climbing activity is excellent for the physical development of the child. However, it also provides an excellent opportunity for children to learn about the joy in exploring on their own.

Climbing means children can get to more places and explore more things. They can climb up on a chair to see how the faucets work in the sink. They can climb up to see out of the window. Climbing extends the range of what children can get into. It is exciting for children to learn of these *extra* possibilities.

2. Parents can provide

It will be exciting for you, too, but perhaps in another way. Some parents develop a great deal of anxiety. They are afraid that their child will fall and get hurt. Some parents get worried about household objects that might receive damage. However, there are fairly simple remedies. You can teach your child how to climb safely. For example, children can be shown how to back down off the bed or couch, back down the stairs, etc. When there are perches that must be forbidden, be firm and consistent (see pp. 104–106). A very important remedy will be to give your child lots of opportunity to climb while under your sensible supervision. Set aside times of the day when you will be right there as your child practices on the stairs. Build a slide for the back yard and teach your child how to use it.

You can also use wide boards and incline one end. Be there as your child learns to climb up the inclined board. You cannot prevent all minor mishaps but you can prevent major ones. You can grab the high chair before it crashes down on top of your child. You can stop your child from falling down the stairs.

Once you have arranged things for safe climbing, you can concentrate on helping your child learn that there is joy in exploring independently. See to it that there are interesting things to explore when your child climbs. A climb up the stairs can be accompanied by putting the clean clothes away, thus giving your child a chance to explore where things are put away. Play "go and fetch" games, such as fetch a toy from the shelf, fetch the soap from the sink, etc. You can play treasure hunt games, too. You hide a treasure for which your child must climb to find. Doing these activities will help your child make a connection between climbing and exploring. Soon your child will learn to use these climbing skills in order to explore and learn new things independently.

3. Feedback

Reinforce your child's independent explorations. Games such as those already mentioned are fun if the child experiences your enjoyment. Praise every new object which your child finds. Even if the discovery seems commonplace or inconsequential to you, the exploration is special to your child. Reinforce the joy of discovery and join in the fun. Your reinforcement is the way to develop in your child the basic outlook of the joy of learning.

Awareness of Self
12–15 Months

A STEP CHILDREN CAN TAKE
To learn that it is fun to
explore new skills

SPECIFIC ABILITY NO. 5
They can feed themselves
with their fingers

1. What this ability means to children

Finger-feeding is a step along the way toward your more sophisticated way of eating with fork, knife, and spoon. Finger-feeding helps a child develop necessary finger dexterity. Your child needs a great deal of practice. Watch as your child intently works to pick up a small piece of food, and think of the satisfaction that is felt as the small muscles in those once clumsy fingers are brought into control. You have an opportunity to provide a rich learning environment for your child.

2. Parents can provide

Provide a variety of finger foods with interesting textures, colors, and shapes. You might offer your child small strips or cubes of cooked potatoes and carrots; small round foods like peas, or oyster crackers; or a special treat of small candies. Dry cereal in its own small box or in a cup is great fun. Some children like crackers they can crumble. Never mind the mess. The little crumbs are fun to pick up one by one.

3. Feedback

You do, no doubt, want your child to eventually use a fork and spoon. Children will when they are ready. For the present, relax and enjoy the finger-feeding stage. Your child enjoys this stage more if you enjoy it, too. Remember, you want your child to learn that it is fun to practice this new ability to use fingers in picking up small objects. Practicing this new ability is like a new adventure to your child. So put aside your distaste for messiness and take the adventure with your child. Praise your child. Reinforce the fun. As your child experiences this fun, a positive basic outlook is being learned. Your child is experiencing the joy of learning and receiving a very early lesson in self-confidence and independence. Remember, you were always depended upon to feed your baby. Now, your child is becoming a somebody who can do things independently. Did you realize that finger-feeding was all this important?

Here are some suggestions you might want to use to increase your child's enjoyment of this learning experience:

Play find the raisins in the cereal.

Have a box or bag for your child to reach into for "surprises" to eat.

Invite your child to peek under your hands to find a hidden cracker.

Have your child reach in your pocket to find a small treat.

Awareness of Self
12–15 Months

A STEP CHILDREN CAN TAKE
To learn that it is fun to explore new skills

SPECIFIC ABILITY NO. 6
They can pick up a toy, release it, and pick it up again

1. What this ability means to children

Picking up a toy, releasing it, and picking it up again may not sound very exciting to you. However, to your child, that ability to *release* is very tricky until it is mastered. Roll a ball and watch what happens when your child tries to roll it back. There is apt to be trouble letting go. Your child will be learning the muscle control necessary to release by endlessly practicing picking things up, releasing them, picking them up again, releasing, etc. When you understand what is going on when children drop food and toys from the high chair, drop toys over the side of the playpen, or drop anything they can lay their hands on from tables and shelves, you will realize how necessary this practice is to your child. The lesson is learning to *release*. You have an opportunity, again, to provide a rich learning environment.

2. Parents can provide

Your child will delight in blocks, balls, soft toys, boxes to drop things in, rings to stack. Why not give your child a low drawer, cupboard, or shelf filled with toys which can be dropped, again and again. Provide your child with room enough to throw a stuffed animal, go after it, throw it again, and go after it. Play roll-the-ball back and forth in a fun game. Praise your child as rings are put one by one on a peg. Make a game of releasing clothespins one by one into a box. Pick up and put toys away together. Outdoors there are pebbles to pick up, hand to you, take back and drop on the ground. Your child may delight in throwing a small pillow, burying a face in it, then throwing it again.

All these games afford your child practice in this new-found ability to release.

3. Feedback

Make these experiences fun, and your child also will be learning positive basic outlooks.

Perhaps you have never thought of learning to release as a lesson in self-confidence and independence. That may be because you take the matter of releasing for granted. Probably, you can no longer remember when release was impossible for you. However, it's a new experience for your child. Learning to release shows children that they can control objects around them, and that it is fun to learn new skills.

Awareness of Self
15–18 Months

A STEP CHILDREN CAN TAKE
To begin learning to de-velop self-confidence

SPECIFIC ABILITY NO. 7
They can drink from a cup

1. What this ability means to children

Children take a while to master this skill so be prepared for lots of spilling. At first, children are apt to grasp the cup in both hands. They tilt the cup more than it needs to be tilted. When you stop and think about it, you will realize that drinking from a cup requires a great deal of coordination between hands, mouth, and head. Gradually, children learn. The hand hold is replaced by holding the cup between thumb and forefinger or with the tips of the fingers. Then, the excessive tilting problem begins to be remedied. Eventually, your child will learn to drink from a cup quite neatly. However, it may take several months, so be patient and understanding.

Your patience and understanding may be tested by something other than the messiness. Many children this age are extremely self-assertive about cup drinking. They may refuse your well-intentioned help and insist upon wielding the cup by themselves. But when children refuse help, remember they are not testing parents, they are really only testing themselves. Children need to know just what they can do for and by themselves. As children succeed in drinking from a cup, they will be gaining self-confidence.

2. Parents can provide

Your child is going to need a great deal of practice in order to master this skill of drinking from a cup. You can provide the opportunities for lots of practice. Offer new and interesting drinks to encourage your child to keep trying. Provide bibs to protect your child, and places to practice where spills are easy to clean up. Fill cups only half full so that they are easier to manage. There are cups on the market designed to reduce spillage. You may want to use these at first, but eventually you will want your child to use regular cups.

Be patient and understanding, of course. Don't be too sensitive when your child refuses your help. Children often refuse help at the beginning of a meal, but as they tire toward the end of the meal, they may signal for help.

3. Feedback

Just learning to drink from a cup alone may be all your child needs to build self-confidence. But why not sweeten the learning with your praise and interest. Show your delight when your child does something independently. Do not push drinking without spilling before your child's developing coordination warrants your expectations. But do applaud successes and even partial successes. Praise will encourage your child to keep trying. Some children like to be told they are growing up. "Big girl," or "Big boy" appeals to some but not to all children. "You did it yourself" may be rewarding. You can even try a small gift when your child "graduates" to full use of a cup. Your research of what works with your child is your challenge. When you effectively demonstrate your satisfaction with your child's ability to drink from a cup without help, your child's self-confidence will be strengthened.

Awareness of Self
15–18 Months

A STEP CHILDREN CAN TAKE
To begin learning to develop self-confidence

SPECIFIC ABILITY NO. 8
They can take off their shoes

1. What this ability means to children

Most children learn how to take off their clothes before they learn how to put them on. Dressing, after all, requires skills in perception, quite a bit of coordination, and some pretty advanced finger dexterity. But taking off shoes is one of the easier skills. Lots of children start here as they begin to want to do more and more for themselves.

Some children must be physically held in order to get them dressed. The reason is that they are interested in so many things that they strain to be on their way about their own business. Getting dressed is a bother. Dressing is too hard for them to do by themselves, yet they don't appreciate having it done for (to) them.

Your child is learning to take off shoes all alone without your interference. What a boost to the ego! It is an early lesson in developing self-confidence.

2. Parents can provide

Give your child the opportunity to practice this new skill. You may have to provide a bit of patience, too, because the shoes may come off time and time again and you are the one who has to put them back on.

It will take a bit of your time, but why not make a game of it with your child. Each of you take off your shoes. You put them all back on for both of you and then start over. You might even be able to effect a trade. Let your child take off shoes and you will put them on if your child will let you also put another article of clothing on.

3. Feedback

Show that you are pleased that your child is learning to do something independently. In just a few months your child will be able to get dressed alone. If you enjoy the achievements along the way, you will help your child develop self-confidence. And that, in turn, will make self dressing proceed more smoothly.

Awareness of Self
15–18 Months

A STEP CHILDREN CAN TAKE
To begin learning to de-
velop self-confidence

SPECIFIC ABILITY NO. 9
They can throw a ball,
although crudely

1. What this ability means to children

Your child can throw a ball with "a casting motion." It
looks pretty funny, and many children can only throw a
ball up. Later, they learn to throw out. It's that tricky business of being able to release objects again. Now, releasing
must be coordinated with the casting motion. That's not
easy. Think what it must mean to children when they have
success with this difficult throwing skill. They are learning
to make an object follow their directions. They are learning that they can be in control. You can help them learn
this skill.

2. Parents can provide

The first things to provide, of course, are balls and
places to throw them. Next, provide some of your time.
Children love to play with balls, but they like it even better
with an adult. Expect that "casting motion" at first, but
gradually you can guide your child to better throwing
skills. You will need patience, of course, and adults are apt
to tire of a primitive ball game long before their child has
had enough. Your games together will be easier for you if
you provide variety.

Experiment with different balls. Medium sized, soft balls

are good indoors. Smaller balls or very large balls are good outdoors. Different colors may make balls more attractive to your child. There are light foam-rubber balls on the market as well.

Now, for those primitive ball games. You will have to research what games are best for your child. You might start with a game where your child throws a ball in your general direction, and you hand it back. You see, catching is even more difficult than throwing, and you'd best concentrate on one skill at a time rather than two skills at once. Then, the game of back-and-forth with a bounce or two in between can be tried. You can work up to games of aiming, though don't expect very much. A child can throw to try to hit a tree. Tossing a ball into something large like a wastebasket is another game.

3. Feedback

Do not try games at which your child will fail because your aim is to let your child succeed. Then, you can reinforce that success. Observe and evaluate just how your child's throwing skill is developing. Don't push beyond these limits. You are trying to build your child's self-confidence and your praise for successes will work wonders.

Awareness of Self
15–18 Months

A STEP CHILDREN CAN TAKE
To begin learning to develop self-confidence

SPECIFIC ABILITY NO. 10
They can stack 3 blocks

1. What this ability means to children

A child with the rudiments of releasing a grasped object can put one block on top of another (see p. 65). But around eighteen months most children have sufficiently matured in their small muscle control to add that third block without knocking the second block off the tower. This is an exciting achievement. Imagine being able to do something you have never been able to do before! You probably will notice that now, instead of horizontal buildings, your child will probably prefer the vertical, tower building. That is like the child saying by behavior, "See, now I can build up. I can make those blocks do what I want them to do. And I can do it myself." This is another early lesson in developing your child's self-confidence.

2. Parents can provide

Your child probably has had blocks around before, but here is a word of caution. The day you see that first three-block tower, do not run to the store for more blocks. It will be some time yet before a four-block tower can be made, and, if you push your child, frustration and failure will be experienced. It is not quantity of blocks that parents can provide. In fact, keep the number down to only three at a time until you are sure that your child is ready for more. However, you can provide the quality of the building materials. Here, again, you will have to experiment. Some children like big blocks, some children like little blocks, some like one color, some like different colors. Some children like all kinds (three at a time). Watch your child and discover what is best to provide for practicing building towers.

You can also provide time. Most children like to practice with their blocks by themselves. What they do not like is being dragged off for a meal, a nap, or a walk in the middle of their activity. Who does? When you see your child deeply engrossed in building something, try not to interrupt. If you must interrupt, do it with consideration. You might say, "In a few minutes, supper will be ready," or "Finish your tower and we will go to the store." Then your child is forewarned.

A few children need to be encouraged to develop this skill of stacking blocks. If your child is one of these, take the time to play "building towers" together. Alternate who puts a block in place. Try building your tower next to your child's, but do not compete. Show your child different things to stack. Let your child show you, too.

3. Feedback

No doubt, that first three-block tower will receive your attention and praise. Continue to praise your child in order to encourage continued practicing of this skill. Your praise will also build self-confidence. Praise, of course, comes in many forms. You will have to determine what kind of praise works best for your child. For some, just a few words will be enough; in fact, more intense accolades might be overpowering. Some children respond to applause and clapping. You can invite another person to "come see." You can display the tower prominently. Try a tower poster on the refrigerator door where you paste a Tower Picture for each time a tower is built. Whatever the feedback your child receives from you, if it is positive and rewarding to your son or daughter, it will help develop self-confidence.

Awareness of Self
15–18 Months

A STEP CHILDREN CAN TAKE	*SPECIFIC ABILITY NO. 11*
To learn that it is fun to	They can start, stop, and
explore their independence	start again, as they walk

1. What this ability means to children

Skills of locomotion require a great deal of practice. Starting, stopping, and starting again are an advance over the clumsy walking when children overran their feet. Balance and coordination are much better now. Your child can learn ways to use walking and running, such as starting and stopping. At this stage children's locomotion is more or less in a straight line. If you observe carefully, you will probably discover that your child cannot turn corners yet—that will come later.

Most children at this age will insist on walking rather than being pushed in a stroller. They are curious and they will dart into all the byways they can. You can expect sudden bursts of locomotion on your walks with your child. That is fine, particularly if your child has *fun* exploring this new stopping and starting skill.

2. Parents can provide

Your child will need plenty of opportunity for practice. You will have to provide safeguards; after all, you cannot let your child dart out into a street. You may even have to use a harness when your walks are along busy streets. You probably will have an enclosed area in the backyard if you live in a neighborhood with a great deal of traffic. Then your child can practice at home. However, do take some walks to the park or wherever you can safely give your child free rein to dart here and there, finding how good it is to develop locomotion skills.

There are a number of games you can play with your child in order to practice starting and stopping:

1. March along together with first one, then the other giving the commands "start" and "stop."

2. Adapt the game of Giant Steps or Captain May I. In order to tag you, your child must stop whenever you say "stop" and start again whenever you say "start."

3. Play Simon Says on your walks.

4. "1, 2, 3, Red Light" is fun.

3. Feedback

Praise and encourage your child to practice the stopping and starting skill. Just the fun of games together will be reward enough if your child sees that you enjoy the game and delight in the exploration of this new-found skill. These are early lessons in helping your child discover that exploring, learning, and discovering independence is fun.

Awareness of Self
15–18 Months

A STEP CHILDREN CAN TAKE
To learn that it is fun to explore their independence

SPECIFIC ABILITY NO. 12
They can lug, tug, push, pull, dump, and pound

1. What this ability means to children

Did you know you have a furniture mover in the family? One fine day you may find your child happily rocking in a rocking chair in the kitchen when you could have sworn that the rocking chair was in the living room. Or you may catch your child in the act of lugging, tugging, pushing, and pulling a high chair over to the sink in order to climb into the sink. Children move all sorts of other things, pulling open drawers and cupboards and happily dumping contents into a play pen. They often insist upon all these activities because self-assertion is very common now. Through these activities children test themselves in order to find out what they can do on their own. The coordination of large muscles is improving rapidly and all a child's active pushing and pulling help. Children can learn the fun of exploring their new powers if you can just put up with this active stage with good grace.

2. Parents can provide

You can buy large toy trucks for pushing along the floor or any number of colorful pull toys. Your child probably will love them. A rocking horse appeals to many children. However, there's another approach to consider. You may have a youngster who is bursting with energy, who is self-assertive, who needs opportunities for developing large muscles. What are the pushing-pulling opportunities in your daily routine in which your child can push and pull constructively? Here are some possibilities:

1. Your child can help push the grocery cart with you when you shop.
2. Your child can push the laundry cart while you hang up clothes.
3. Your child can push the vacuum cleaner.
4. Your child can pull open drawers for you as you put the clean clothes away.
5. Your child can help you push furniture that you want moved.

6. Your child can push the stroller on your walks.
7. Your child can push a little mop or shovel beside your mop or shovel, imitating you in your tasks.

The list could go on and on. Be on the lookout for other opportunities. Working with you will add to your child's pleasure.

You can also make up games. Some children like to push a sibling in the carriage and even take turns pushing and being pushed. Do you have a TV stand on wheels that isn't being used? You can decorate this to make a train, a ship, or a car, that your child can push.

3. Feedback

Praise your child for each new activity, as long as it is safe and nondestructive. You will particularly want to praise your child for whatever attempts are made at household tasks. Respect the self-assertiveness and enjoy with your child the growing sense of independence. Your joy will reinforce your child's joy in exploring all these new activities.

Awareness of Self
15–18 Months

A STEP CHILDREN CAN TAKE
To learn that it is fun to explore their independence

SPECIFIC ABILITY NO. 13
They can stoop to pick things up

1. What this ability means to children

Children are delighted when they learn to stoop and squat. It was not long ago that they struggled to get up on their feet and stand alone. Now, balance and coordination are good enough for them to both stand and squat and still remain on their own two feet. That is progress. They may practice this skill endlessly. Many children love to look between their legs upside down. That looks funny to adults, but to a youngster, it is a new way of seeing things.

Children are curious. They explore by touching and feeling. Once they can stoop, there are more interesting objects to touch and feel than ever before. This is an age of constant stooping to pick things up, to explore things more closely. A walk around the block with your child may seem like an endless task because of the constant interruptions to stop, stoop, and pick things up. However, think what it means to your child to be independently able to so expand the range of explorations.

2. Parents can provide

You can give your young explorer the opportunity and time to explore new fields. Take walks to new places. Also, there is much that can be accomplished right at home. If you want to encourage your child to stoop and explore, you might want to "seed" an area with interesting things to be picked up. Place pieces of velveteen, round balls, smooth plastic paperweights, pieces of sandpaper, under chairs and tables. Tell your child to stoop and look for these treasures. Children love feeling new surfaces and shapes. Of course, your child may be more encouraged by edible treasures. Experiment with all kinds of treasures to encourage your child to stoop and explore.

Besides a treasure hunt, there are other games to try. Adapt Simon Says and Follow the Leader for calisthenics games of "stand" and "squat" that you can play together.

3. Feedback

When your child stoops to pick things up that are interesting, this is your cue to show interest and enthusiasm. A wiggly worm may not be your idea of a marvelous discovery, but it may be to your child. Try to show understanding and respect by putting yourself in your child's shoes. Of course, there will be times when the object presented you will be unacceptable. You are not expected to accept a dirty cigar butt and your diplomacy will be called upon. But do work up enthusiasm for shells, pebbles, leaves, no matter how ordinary or numerous. You will be encouraging your child to perfect stooping and squatting skills. And your child will be learning the fun of exploring new-found independence.

Awareness of Self
15–18 Months

A STEP CHILDREN CAN TAKE
To learn that it is fun to
explore their independence

SPECIFIC ABILITY NO. 14
They can run, although
stiffly

1. What this ability means to children

Most children at this developmental level are really quite steady on their feet. Walking skills have matured so that each step glides more than the previous pick-up-a-foot, move-it, and put-it-down again steps. Running is really only a fast walk and rather awkward at that. But children, at this level, seem to love to try running. Running is a way to assert their newfound independence. They are charged with energy; they dart here and there. They cannot turn corners at a run yet. They have to stop and then turn.

They probably do not run in order to get to a place faster, for fast or slow, the relationship to time has little meaning to them at this early age. They run just for the joy of the action and because running is one more way to explore their budding independence.

2. Parents can provide

Provide your child with opportunities to run, safeguarded by you, of course. You can make up running games that work best with your child, but here are some suggestions:

1. Have your child run and fetch (do errands for you).
2. Have your child run and hide. Most children love simple hide-and-seek games.
3. Play at chase and being chased. This activity is loved by most children. Some can even weather the tension of "I'm going to get you." Other children cannot, though, so experiment gently.
4. Play tag.
5. Run races.

You might as well give up the idea that your walks will be from here to there in a straight line. Your child will dart into this path or that alleyway. Some neighbor's front steps may need to be climbed before you can go on. Put up with these diversions good naturedly because your child needs to explore and discover what independence is all about.

3. Feedback

Make running fun for your child. You can do this by enjoying games and walks with your child. Show your delight that your child is able to run. Praise the explorations. Your child might like a badge with a picture of a runner on it or pictures of runners on a bulletin board. Just the laughter and good times of running together may be encouragement enough.

Awareness of Self
18–24 Months

A STEP CHILDREN CAN TAKE
To learn that independence
is worthwhile

SPECIFIC ABILITY NO. 15
They can turn single pages
of a book by themselves

1. What this ability means to children

Try turning the pages of a book, yourself, and see what goes into this skill. Turning pages, singly, takes a great deal of finger dexterity and a flexible wrist. Previously, your child did not have that dexterity and the wrist was stiffer than it is now. Your child could turn pages, but bunches of pages got turned at one time. You were depended upon to turn the single pages when you read together. At this stage, children can turn single pages by themselves and that is quite an accomplishment. Most children love to imitate adults reading. They will sit for quite long periods of time "reading" a book, turning the pages one at a time, and perhaps even "reading" out loud. It is important to them to be so grown up.

However, do not be entirely fooled! Your child is probably not past the tearing-pages-out stage. Tearing, after all, is fun. However, you can teach what your child is permitted to tear and what is not to be torn.

2. Parents can provide

Now is the time for children to have some books of their own. You may want to start out with heavy cardboard books and cloth books which have pages that cannot be torn. The tearing urge can be satisfied by the pile of old magazines you keep in a special place for your child. Make sure your child knows that old magazines can be torn but books must not be torn.

When you settle down to read a bedtime story, let your child turn the pages for you. This will help your son or daughter feel important. See to it that your child has opportunities to look at books and "read" alone. Some children like books nearby when they wake in the morning. Many like to look at picture books when their parents are reading the paper.

Try different kinds of books until you find those that your child likes enough to turn each page singly without your help. That way your child is learning that independence is worthwhile.

3. Feedback

Your child will learn that independently turning the pages is worthwhile, particularly if you show that you approve and take delight in that new skill. Praise and encourage your child's practicing turning pages.

Awareness of Self
18–24 Months

A STEP CHILDREN CAN TAKE
To learn that independence
is worthwhile

SPECIFIC ABILITY NO. 16
They can take off their
shoes, hat, mittens, and
even unzip zippers

1. What this ability means to children

Taking clothes off is easier than putting clothes on. Most children learn to undress before they can dress. But it is all part of learning to do things for themselves. At this developmental level, most children take an active interest in dressing and undressing. A few months previously, dressing was a battle. But now most children cooperate. They will hold their legs up for pants to be put on. They will plunge their arms into sleeves held ready for them. They are interested in the whole process and try to learn to take care of themselves.

At this level, most children will practice the skills required to undress themselves. When they are alone, they quite often take off all their clothes, and it is not uncommon to see a naked twenty-one-month-old child darting outdoors. That's independence for you!

2. Parents can provide

You can provide opportunities for your child to practice undressing. This is hard for some parents to do. They watch their child struggling to get a coat off and instantly go to help the child. That really is not much help in the long run, however. You will need to watch your child carefully so that you can gauge when to help and when to wait. Do not let the frustration level get too high, but do give your child a chance to undress unaided.

When the undressing skills are practiced in the back yard or otherwise in public, use some care in handling the matter. If you shame your child, you will lose ground on the "independence is worthwhile" goal. On the other hand, public exposure is rather frowned upon. All that may be necessary is to point out that grownups undress only in special places such as their bedrooms or the bathroom. This puts the emphasis on positive aspects of growing up.

You can also control public nudity by giving your child attention and practice-session time indoors. Make up undressing games that make undressing fun. Silly rhymes, jingles, and songs delight most children. Here is an example:

> First the shoes, then the socks
> And next the pants come off;
> Then the sweater and next your shirt,
> Soon you're down to your skin so soft.

You can buy cloth books and practice-boards that have zippers to unzip, buttons to unbutton, shoelaces to unlace right on them. However, you really do not have to buy expensive toys. Do you have a suitcase that unzips? This is an excellent zipper for beginning to learn to unzip. Your child may delight in unzipping zippers for you as zipping and unzipping skills increase. Before you throw away or give away old clothing, inspect it for practice materials— buttons and buttonholes, shoes and shoelaces, snaps and hooks. You probably have all sorts of practice equipment on hand that your child will enjoy.

3. Feedback

Show your pleasure as your child learns more and more undressing skills and self-help skills. Praise and encourage your child for each new skill that is learned. Do not push too fast or too hard, however, for this could cause your child unnecessary frustration and even failures. That would not help toward the goal that "independence is worthwhile." Observe your child's progress and praise the successes. You can try stars on a chart to reward successes. For example, when you are sure your child can manage taking off bluejeans, make a chart of the days of the week and glue a star for each day that part of undressing is accomplished. Or, try a flannelgraph with the figure of a child and the articles of clothing your child is able to take off. Let your child undress the figure as your child's undressing procceds. Part of your research is to find out what is most rewarding to your child.

Awareness of Self
18–24 Months

A STEP CHILDREN CAN TAKE
To learn that independence
is worthwhile

SPECIFIC ABILITY NO. 17
They can ask to go to the
toilet, either verbally
or by gestures

1. What this ability means to children

There is a way to go about toilet-training that can accomplish the goal "independence is worthwhile." First of all, children can be allowed to train themselves. If parents praise their children's efforts to do things for themselves, most children will try to be independent as soon as they can. One early attempt at independence is asking to go to the toilet. Children need parental help with much of the procedure, but asking for it gives them some small measure of control over the situation.

Secondly, parents can relax and let nature take its course. Think about the whole toilet-training subject from a child's point of view. Only very gradually do children realize that they can control their bladder and bowels. Sphincter muscles must mature. Until the maturation occurs children do not have control and are unaware that they ever will. Children must also understand the relationship of the toilet to urine or feces. Diapers always took care of body wastes before. What progress when children realize that urine and feces belong in the toilet and they are the ones who can deposit them there themselves! Eventually, children realize all the components of toileting. Their bodies mature and they have family members to watch and imitate. As children are encouraged to be independent and are reinforced for progress, they will toilet-train themselves. What a wonderful way to learn that independence is worthwhile!

2. Parents can provide

You can provide a relaxed atmosphere, follow your child's lead, give every chance for independent action, but help when help is needed. Progress will depend on your sensitive handling of what your child can do and what is still not possible. For example, your child has indicated a wish to go to the toilet by coming to you with diapers off and in hand. Fine! That part was done independently. You are alert enough to follow up the request. You go to the bathroom with your child. The potty or toilet seat is ready. You help your child on only if help is needed. Otherwise, let your child climb on the toilet seat. You will probably need to help with wiping, but let your child unroll the toilet paper. You will have to help in re-dressing, but let your child climb to the sink and turn on the faucet to wash up. There are lots of opportunities in toileting for your child to learn that independence is worthwhile.

3. Feedback

Praise each step of progress your child makes toward taking care of toileting. Give help when asked and give it willingly, but encourage independent efforts. You might as well expect regressions and certainly expect lots of accidents. When you have had a dry week, don't get discouraged if the next two are wet. Often, children suddenly seem toilet-trained on a visit to grandmother's, only to "regress" when they get home and relax. Overlook the failures and keep your attention focused on successes. Be careful not to shame your child in any way. You can achieve a trained child by shaming, to be sure; but quite likely a shamed child does not learn that independence is worthwhile.

Awareness of Self
18–24 Months

A STEP CHILDREN CAN TAKE
To begin learning to recognize their selfhood

SPECIFIC ABILITY NO. 18
They can learn "I," "you," "me," and "mine"

1. What this ability means to children

Pronouns are one of the last parts of speech to be used by a child. In learning to talk, children use nouns first, then verbs; later they use adjectives and adverbs, and finally, prepositions and pronouns. As was pointed out in chapter 1, the extremely egocentric one-year-old does not distinguish between self and others; everything is self. Of what use is "I" and "you," "me" and "mine?" As children move through the second year of life, however, they become aware that each is an "I" as distinguished from another person who is a "you." Children also begin to have a rudimentary sense of possession. They take an interest in what belongs to people, particularly what belongs to themselves. Then "me" and "mine" make sense. Children at this level of development are very apt to hoard whatever they can put their hands on, not because they need things, but rather, for the good feeling of possession. "It's mine" is a commonly repeated phrase. They find it very difficult to share because they are still struggling to understand what belongs to them. They really must learn about what belongs to them before they can be expected to understand what belongs to others. Most children do not begin to share until their third year of life. However, all these concepts will gradually be understood as children discover their own selfhood.

2. Parents can provide

Let us start with the language development before discussing possessions. You will realize, however, that both proceed together. Understanding the words depends on the experience of possessing.

Children learn words they hear others using. They imitate. Be sure you are a good model. Pronounce clearly and correctly. Gestures accompanying your words are very important. When you say, "I am washing my hands," point to yourself with "I" and "my," and to your hands with "hands." When you say, "You wash your hands," point to your child and your child's hands.

Next, consider possessions. Parents can give children toys that belong only to them and to no one else. Children will appreciate their own shelf or their own drawer or toy chest that are for their possessions and no one else's. As children realize that their possessions are respected and really are theirs, then they can begin to appreciate that other people also have things that belong just to them.

Sharing toys with other children may present a problem. Children find it much easier to share with adults, because adults return toys on demand. Children the age of your child do not share—they are hoarders. It is not a good idea to force your child to share with another child. Forced sharing confuses children's perception of possessions and what belongs to them. You might keep a cache of a few toys, not your child's, that you can draw upon when little visitors appear.

There are any number of simple games you can play to combine the idea of possessions with language practice. As you point to your child's possessions, let your child repeat the name of the article and say "It's mine." Then point to something of your own for the response of "Yours." Make up flash cards with pictures of possessions for your child to sort into a "mine" and a "yours" pile. Some children delight in a little suitcase made of cardboard and filled with pictures of their special possessions.

3. Feedback

Praise correct use of words. Respect your child's property rights so that eventually your property rights and the rights of others will be respected. Try to remember that awareness of self as distinct from others is still just dawning and that your child must go through this stage before any real concern for other people can be felt. As children learn that they have possessions, they will feel good about themselves. This is necessary for children to learn so that eventually they will feel good about other people.

Awareness of Self
18–24 Months

A STEP CHILDREN CAN TAKE
To begin learning to recognize their selfhood

SPECIFIC ABILITY NO. 19
They can refer to themselves by name

1. What this ability means to children

Part of the whole complicated process of discovering selfhood occurs when children learn that they have a name of their own. It is almost as though children must stand outside themselves and look at themselves from the outside in. This is not a simple accomplishment at all when you realize that just a few months earlier your child was so "locked in egocentricity" that little could be perceived except self. Learning to refer to themselves by name, as well as learning that other people have names, will help children distinguish people as individuals, including themselves as individuals.

2. Parents can provide

When you refer to your child, use a given name. Instead of "Let's go to the grocery store," try "Lynn, you and I will go to the grocery store." Instead of "Wash your hands," try "Please wash your hands, Kim."

Tell stories using your child's name for the central character. Most children love to hear their name in a story. When you read stories together, try substituting your child's name instead of using the name in the book.

When you write your child's letter to grandmother, show where you have signed your child's name.

Show baby snapshots you have taken, always referring to your child by name as you point out the people in the pictures. Make a game of naming people, including your child: a "who is that" game, but insist on names.

Some children love little songs. Feel free to change words to suit your own purposes. For example, in "Ring-around-the-Rosy," change "all fall down" to "Dale falls down."

Once you get into the swing of working on names with your child, you will discover all sorts of ways to provide opportunities to use names, particularly your child's name.

3. Feedback

When children use their own name, parents should show delight. You will find that the naming games and the stories and songs are fun. Your enjoyment with your child will be reinforcing. Avoid making fun of any particular names or making fun of your child in this sensitive period when Selfhood is beginning to be discovered. You will want your child to feel good about self. Children deserve respect as valuable individuals in their own right.

Awareness of Self
18–24 Months

A STEP CHILDREN CAN TAKE	SPECIFIC ABILITY NO. 20
To begin learning to recognize their selfhood	They can distinguish between what belongs to their own person (e.g., legs, eyes, nose, hair) and to themselves as persons (e.g. hat, shoes, shirt)

1. What this ability means to children

Children at this age are beginning to attain a rudimentary sense of personal identity and personal possession. They are interested in the parts of their own body as parts of themselves. One-year-old children are interested in their hands because they want to know what can be done with them. But now, children are interested in their hands as part of themselves. They are also beginning to realize that clothes belong to them, too, but not as part of their bodies. They take a new interest in clothes, rather than just tolerating them as they did previously. Your child will need your help in making all these distinctions because they are important in the struggle to learn about selfhood. Your child is gradually getting to know a self who is an individual distinct from other individual people. What a discovery! It is important to your child's future to feel good about this self.

2. Parents can provide

Naming games will help your child to distinguish between parts of the body and the clothes that are possessions. You might begin naming parts of the body.

The simplest games are pointing to parts of the body and naming the name of each part. Point to your eyes and say "eye." Ask your child to do the same. Start with only a few body parts, but then gradually add more. You may find your child will make a ritual of naming parts before naptime or at bedtime. If pointing does not work, try a flannelgraph on which your child can add eyes, ears, etc., to the outlined figure as the parts are named.

When parts of the body can be named correctly, you can expand the games to include what the parts do. Your child probably has played "peek-a-boo" and knows that when you cover your eyes, you cannot see. Eyes are for seeing. Put your hands over your child's ears. Then, tell your child to stop you from hearing. Ears are for hearing. Tell your child to stop you from talking. Your child probably will enjoy covering your mouth. A mouth is for talking. Your child is learning the words "see," "hear," "talk." You can teach the words "smell," and "taste" in a similar fashion. Your child will not only learn words, but will learn about the body and the parts of that body that belong to self.

The names of articles of clothing can be learned by pointing games, too. Point to your child's shirt and say "This is Donny's———" and let your child supply "shirt." As you go through dressing and undressing routines, use the names of the clothing articles. Find pictures of clothes and play naming games with them. But you can go further than just naming games. Many parents involve their child in the laundry procedures. Children soon learn to put their soiled clothes in the hamper. They love to put their clean clothes away. Many of them can even fold their clean clothes. Involving children in the care of their clothes tends to make the clothes take on new importance.

3. Feedback

You will want to encourage correct use of words by praising your child for success in the naming games. Show how pleased you are when your child cares for clothes and helps you with the laundry. Communicate that you think the parts of your child's body and the clothes that belong to your child's self are important. As your child begins to recognize self as distinct from others, you can help by showing how important your child's self is to you.

Awareness of the Environment
12–15 Months

A STEP CHILDREN CAN TAKE
A growing enthusiasm for learning about the world in which they live

SPECIFIC ABILITY NO. 1
They can make a mark on paper with a crayon

1. What this ability means to children

One of the ways very young children become aware of their world is by learning about the objects around them and what they can do with these objects. They cannot learn much until their maturing coordination allows them to manipulate the objects. So think what it must mean to your child whose fingers now have the fine muscle control to grasp a crayon. The first mark a child makes with a crayon will be quite an accomplishment. This can be an early opportunity for your child to be enthusiastic about the world and the objects in it.

At first children draw lines every which way, sometimes covering the entire paper. Circular motions will come later. Crude pictures meant to represent something come much later. At this age, the process of scribbling on the paper is what engages the child, not making a picture. Two or three years will pass before you have any basis for predicting artistic talent, so relax and encourage your child's enthusiastic scribbling. Your child is learning about the environment.

2. Parents can provide

The first things to provide, of course, are crayons and paper. Crayons are suggested because they are fatter and easier to manipulate than skinny pencils. Children can use pencils a little later. Provide plenty of paper in strategic places so that your scribbler won't have to use the walls or mirrors. In fact, some parents find that it helps to keep large sheets of fresh paper taped to the refrigerator door or to other accessible surfaces where the child is permitted and encouraged to scribble uninhibited.

You may want to play scribble games with your child—first you put a mark on the paper, then your child puts a mark on the paper, now your turn, then, your child's turn. Children love to imitate. However, do not push beyond scribbles until your child is ready. If you push too hard or too fast, your child will experience failures rather than receive an early lesson in enthusiasm about the environment.

3. Feedback

Encourage your child as this skill of marking with a crayon on paper develops. Show your delight in any accomplishments, meager as they may seem to you. You might even show these first scribbles to other people in order to demonstrate your interest and support. See what kind of praise works best for your child.

Don't be too upset with occasional scribbles on wall-paper or woodwork. After all, the attitudes your child is building are really more important than the interior deco-ration in your home. And it won't take long for your child to learn where you allow scribbling and where you do not allow it. If you consistently praise scribbling on paper and show your disapproval of scribbling elsewhere, your child will soon catch on.

Awareness of the Environment
12–15 Months

A STEP CHILDREN CAN TAKE
A growing enthusiasm for
learning about the world
in which they live

SPECIFIC ABILITY NO. 2
They can stack one block
on top of another

1. What this ability means to children

Young children have difficulty putting one block on top of another block because their clumsy "release" mechanism often causes them to knock both blocks over. It is one thing to grasp a block, but quite another thing to reverse the process and release it. Try it yourself and notice how complicated it is. That release action must be controlled before a child can stack, so bear with your child as this new ability is learned.

Children are also just learning that their blocks are more than just extensions of themselves. Now they can under-stand that the blocks are separate from themselves. Chil-dren learn that they can have some kind of control over the blocks. Even though the control is limited to putting one block on top of another, your child will probably be quite joyful. This new ability will add to your child's growing enthusiasm about the environment. You will want to reinforce that enthusiasm.

2. Parents can provide

Big blocks will be easier to handle than the tiny variety, although your child eventually will want to try stacking small blocks. Provide blocks two at a time for stacking. Three blocks are too many at first. You will have to observe your child in order to ascertain the level of readiness. If you push too fast, unnecessary failures will occur and failures may lead to loss of enthusiasm.

Give your child time to practice. When your child is working intently with blocks, avoid interruptions. Allow enough time for your child to have some measure of success. Most shopping trips, meals, visits, can be delayed a few minutes.

Some children will work with blocks quite happily all by themselves. Other children want an adult working and playing with them. You will have to find out which your child prefers.

3. Feedback

Overlook your child's clumsiness and failures. No one said a one-year-old had to be a master builder. Whenever your child does stack one block on another, no matter how imperfectly, give praise. Show how delighted you are with whatever the success. Your reinforcement will add to your child's enthusiasm about the accomplishment and will have a great deal to do with a positive outlook about the world as perceived by your child.

Awareness of the Environment
12–15 Months

A STEP CHILDREN CAN TAKE
To learn that it is fun
to experiment

SPECIFIC ABILITY NO. 3
They can experiment by
putting an object in a
container and removing it

1. What this ability means to children

Children learn by experimenting. They try this and that to find out what works. They recognize now that objects are separate from themselves, and they now have sufficient manual dexterity to manipulate the objects around them. These maturations make experimenting possible. Every day is an opportunity for children to discover new goals and new means by which to attain them.

Your child does not think in the way you think. A child will not consciously think, "Now if I try this, will I get to that?" Rather, children at this stage are experiencing. They try something and the result of their experiment registers in their experience. Only toward the end of the second year can children, generally, think about results of an action before they act. Now, however, the experiences are building toward that thought process.

Your goal will be to help your child learn that experimenting is fun. So get ready to have fun yourself. The experimenting you can encourage in this case is to have your child put things into a container and then remove them. Some children will do this endlessly. Others can easily be encouraged to try.

2. Parents can provide

Begin with containers that will readily hold all kinds of objects: pails, wastebaskets, drawers, pots and pans can receive clothespins, balls, blocks, etc.

Gradually, as you see that your child is ready, graduate to beads into plastic bottles, plastic straws into a box with a slot in it, raisins into a small raisin box. You don't have to have expensive toys for your child to learn this skill, so use your imagination.

Do not expect your child to have success yet with the toys which have openings of different shapes and pieces which match the openings. These toys require an advanced stage of this skill of putting objects into a container and removing them. Keep at an appropriate level with this skill so that your child will have success.

Play games of putting in and taking out with your child. This will give you an opportunity to observe the progress your child is making so that you can choose the appropriate level. But keep your games fun so that your child will want to continue experimenting.

3. Feedback

Encourage your child's experiments. Your interest in any endeavors will mean a great deal to your child. Show your delight as progress is made and you will be reinforcing the fun aspect in experimenting. This is your opportunity to help your child build the positive basic outlook that learning is a joyful experience.

Awareness of the Environment
12–15 Months

A STEP CHILDREN CAN TAKE
To learn that it is fun
to experiment

SPECIFIC ABILITY NO. 4
They can watch objects
fall as they drop them

1. What this ability means to children

When children deliberately tip their milk so that it pours all over the floor, parents can refrain from anger when they understand that something very important may be taking place. Children at this developmental level watch very carefully where the milk goes. They drop crumbs from their highchair and watch each crumb to see where it lands. They drop their toys over the side of the play pen and, again, watch where each lands. Dropping, followed by observation of results, means you have an "experimenter" on your hands. Your child is not messing up the house to anger you. Your child is experimenting. Rejoice, because experimenting is the way learning proceeds at this age.

Maturations have occurred to make these experiments possible. Your child can grasp *and* release. Visual perception has advanced. Hand and eye movements are becoming coordinated. These new maturations are exciting advances to your child.

2. Parents can provide

Your patience will probably be your biggest contribution. Patience won't be so difficult now that you understand the importance of the experiments. Forget the mess around the high chair. When toys get dropped over the playpen rail, return them so that they can be dropped again, and again. An older child can help in the retrieval system to save you all that stooping to pick things up.

Provide droppable objects of all sizes and shapes. A bean-bag goes zlop, a ball bounces and rolls, a piece of carrot may bump around a bit, and water slurps all over. Think of all the new experiments your child can try. These early dropping experiences are fun.

3. Feedback

Your child will have more fun if you will share your delight. Praise your child for trying new experiments. Just your attention and your providing new objects to drop will be rewarding. But you can also share joy and reward your child's observations. You have an opportunity, too, to teach new words for the results of the experiments: "See, it *bounces.*" "The block goes *down.*" "It went over *there.*" "It *stopped.*" But your main goal is to have your child enjoy experimenting.

Awareness of the Environment
12–15 Months

A STEP CHILDREN CAN TAKE
To learn that it is fun
to experiment

SPECIFIC ABILITY NO. 5
They can manipulate toys
in relation to other toys

1. What this ability means to children

Once children have matured enough to know that their toys are objects separate from themselves, and once they have adequate coordination to manipulate objects, they can play many new games of experimenting. They can bang two objects together to see what kind of noise they make. They can put toys together and take them apart to see how the toys work. They can twist lids, take them off, and put them on again, learning the relationship between lid and container. Think of all the experiments children carry out each day. As children experiment, they experience "fits together," "in," "out," "bigger," "smaller," "comes apart," "makes a noise," etc. These experiences are the way, the only way, children at this early age learn. Try using just words to teach your child the meaning of "bigger" and "smaller." You won't get very far. But demonstrate with measuring cups, for example, while using the words. Let your child see, hear, feel, and do. That's the way children learn, and such learning is fun. You are helping your child build positive outlooks so that learning will always be thought of as fun.

2. Parents can provide

Lots of objects around the house are excellent for practicing this skill: old-fashioned clothespins, containers with lids, nested bowls, plastic cups, and spoons. You might make an inventory of all you have on hand for your child to experiment with before rushing to the store to buy expensive toys.

There are wonderful toys to be bought, of course, but make sure that you do not get ones that are too complex. If your child is only ready for a one-piece puzzle, a three-piece puzzle can be overly frustrating. Start with a wooden or plastic puzzle which has a single piece: a circle, a triangle, a whole animal, a whole piece of fruit, etc. Toys with pegs for stacking rings are excellent. Study your child and study the available toys and match the toys to your child's abilities so that experimentation meets with success and is fun.

Sometimes children will experiment happily on their own. But many times it will be more fun if you will join in the games. "Take turn" games are fun. For example, you place a ring on the stack stick, then your child puts one on, then you, then your child.

Show your child new experiments to try. Probably your child will gladly imitate what you do. Demonstrate how to fit clothespins together. Show how to put the smaller bowl into the larger bowl. Give the words that go with each experiment so that the words can be imitated, too.

3. Feedback

Encourage any kind of experimenting. Then be sure to praise your child when experimenting leads to success. When your child does not succeed, overlook it. You might offer a little help, but essentially let your child find out what fits where or how to get the lid off by independent experimenting.

Your child will feel good as success is experienced. You will add to the fun by showing that what is being accomplished makes you happy, too.

Awareness of the Environment
15–18 Months

A STEP CHILDREN CAN TAKE
To learn the joy of using curiosity to try new combinations

SPECIFIC ABILITY NO. 6
They can throw and go after an object

1. What this ability means to children

The difference between this ability and children's ability to just throw a ball (see p. 39) is that now they go after what is thrown in order to see where it lands. The object may be a stuffed animal, a ball, or a pillow. In addition to developing a motor skill, children are experimenting with what happens as a result of their actions. They are curious to discover what happens when they throw down, up, out, and into. Children must act and then see what the results are. This is the way they learn. Learning is joyful when children use their curiosity.

2. Parents can provide

Since this throwing and going-after ability is so important, why don't you remove breakable objects in rooms where your child can practice? Provide opportunities to throw things both indoors and outdoors. Provide safe objects to throw. Show your child different ways to throw.

There are lots of games to play with your child. You can pitch clothespins into a large basket together. Adapt Simon Says and take turns being Simon who directs, "Simon says throw the ball up. Simon says throw it on the floor. Simon says throw the ball against the wall." Try an adaptation of Follow the Leader, using two balls and taking turns being leader. The follower has to throw the ball where the leader does.

3. Feedback

Encourage your child to go after a thrown object and see the results. Praise your child's being curious. Curiosity is a

precious gift and should be a joy to use. Encourage experimenting and show your delight when your child uses
curiosity in exploring what happens when an object is
thrown.

Awareness of the Environment
15–18 Months

A STEP CHILDREN CAN TAKE
To learn the joy of using
curiosity to try new
combinations

SPECIFIC ABILITY NO. 7
They can first empty and
later on fill

1. What this ability means to children

As children work with emptying and filling, they are
experiencing the concept of volume. These are very early
lessons, to be sure, and it will be several years yet before
they understand volume the way you do. For example, if
you fill a tall thin glass with eight ounces of water and a
short, fat glass with eight ounces of water, your child will
think the tall, thin glass holds more water. This is a normal
mistake for children this young to make. But children
learn that there are different volumes as they empty and
fill different size and shapes of containers. Your child
may spend quite long periods of time using curiosity to
experience volume.

2. Parents can provide

Provide plastic containers of various sizes and shapes for
your child to fill and empty in the bathtub at bathtime.
Show your child how to pour the water from one container

to another. Let your child try it. Use the words "empty," "fill," "pour," "bigger," "smaller," etc.

Later in their development of this skill, most children love to experiment with sand. If you can afford it, by all means make or buy a sandbox and stock it with pails and shovels. Children will shovel different amounts of sand into a pail, dump it out, shovel in, dump out, endlessly. Experimenting with emptying and filling is your child's way of using curiosity to try new combinations and learn by experiencing.

Let your child eventually graduate to sand plus water as a further extension to experimenting with emptying and filling. Wet sand has a new kind of volume for your child to learn about and is a new combination to challenge your child's curiosity.

3. Feedback

Observe carefully. Does your child experiment only when you are together? If so, play games together and praise your child for trying new combinations. Some children will work on emptying and filling by themselves. But somewhere along the line, show that your child's fun delights you, too. This will encourage your child to continue using curiosity and to enjoy experimenting.

Awareness of the Environment
15–18 Months

A STEP CHILDREN CAN TAKE	SPECIFIC ABILITY NO. 8
To begin learning about sequence and relationships	They can learn the names of events and objects that give them pleasure

1. What this ability means to children

When children are getting along pretty well with motor skills, many of them reach a period when they seem to "catch up" on language, particularly those children who reduced talking while they learned how to walk. Assertiveness is another factor at this stage. As children become more independent because of their developing motor skills, they are apt to become very assertive about what they want. And they want what they want *when* they want it. Verbal communication becomes important to them, especially if they cannot get satisfaction for their demands unless they use words.

As children learn names of events and objects that they want, they begin to get a crude perception of sequence of events ("after your nap, we will go outdoors") and relationships between objects ("your toy is up there on the shelf"). They begin to use sequence words such as *before, after, when, now,* and to use relationship words such as *over, under, beside, up there,* in order to get what they want. But children need their parents' help during what may be a difficult period. Many children get terribly frustrated when they begin to use words but still can't pronounce the words understandably. How awful not to be understood, particularly when the asked-for object is wanted immediately! This failure to communicate causes many a temper tantrum. Therefore, help your child with language skills about sequence and relationships in the environment. This is also an early lesson toward the basic outlook that the environment is predictable.

2. Parents can provide

You will be the likely model for your child to imitate. Therefore, be sure to say words clearly, slowly, and correctly. Gestures along with words are very helpful to most children as they learn meanings of words. When you say "the pail is under the chair," point to the pail under the chair. When you say "the book is beside the box," place the book beside the box. Have frequent conversations so that your child has many words and phrases to imitate.

You can't gesture very effectively with sequence words. But your child will gradually learn from experience. However, learning will not occur if you say "after you wash your hands we will have orange juice," and then you forget the juice. If you are answering the telephone and you say "we will play later," be sure to play with your child when you finish your phone conversation.

Try cutting some pictures out of magazines to make flash cards for a game with your child to teach relationship words. One card could be a child under the table, to teach "under." Another card could be the sun in the sky, to teach "up." Two puppies together can teach "beside."

Pairs of pictures can help with the sequence words. One pair might be a child putting on pajamas, then the child in bed listening to a story, to teach "after." Another pair might be a child washing hands, then the child receiving a cookie, to teach "before."

As you read stories to your child, ask simple questions to emphasize the words you are trying to teach. For example, after reading a story about a clown, ask, "What did Mr. Clown do *first*?" "*Then,* what did he do?"

But keep your questions simple and only concentrate on one or two words at a time until your child understands and then can use the words.

3. Feedback

Praise your child as new words are learned. Your child might like stars on a chart for each new word, or if the flash cards worked, award a flash card as each new word is learned. Your child might like a treasure chest for storing the cards. A decorated shoe box, cigar box, or the like can be a treasure chest. Your child may not need these material rewards. Satisfaction at being able to communicate verbally may be reward enough. Study your child to determine the best kind of feedback as awareness of sequence and relationships progresses.

Awareness of the Environment
18–24 Months

A STEP CHILDREN CAN TAKE
To learn that the environment is predictable

SPECIFIC ABILITY NO. 9
They can learn where things are kept

1. What this ability means to children

Something new and important happens to children sometime in the last half of their second year. They begin to be able to think about something without actually having to see the object, person, or event first. This means that they can remember where things are kept. Of course, if you go shifting things around in your home all the time, your child will have difficulty. But if you will keep cereals on one shelf, canned goods on another shelf, and so forth, your child will remember. The drawer for underwear, the drawer for sweaters, and the drawer for pants and shirts will be remembered too.

In fact, at this stage most children want, even demand, orderliness and routine. Their sense of security is enhanced as they learn that everything has its place. They can learn where the groceries go, where the pots and pans are kept, which clean clothes go to whose room, where the dirty clothes belong, where their bib is kept. They are learning to predict where they will find things. These constants will contribute to their later learning about things in the world that are predictable and can be counted upon.

2. Parents can provide

Try to keep a fairly stable household where change is at a minimum. Show your child where things are kept and then always keep them in those locations.

In teaching your child where things are kept, some games may be in order. For example, as you put the groceries away, sing a little jingle like this:

> This is where the cereal goes
> The bread is kept right in here
> And this is where the cans go
> Pop, goes the weasel.

Or try a guessing game in the bedroom:

> Where do we put the shoes?
> Where do sweaters belong?
> Where does your hair brush go?

Praise your child's correct answers. When an answer is incorrect, tell your child to find the right place.

Your child may like a "go and fetch" game. "Get Mommy a sweater" or "Get Daddy's shoes." Keep requests simple and do not make more than two requests at one time because that is probably all your child can remember.

Let your child help you put the groceries away. You have a potential household helper. Your child will learn quite quickly where things are kept if you will be a little patient. Involve your helper gradually in the routines of your house, such as putting dirty clothes in the hamper, getting the frying pan out, finding the clean towels. You

will be amazed at how your child will show you where
things are kept, if you provide the opportunity.

3. Feedback

Help your child to remember where things are kept.
Offer praise when your child remembers correctly. Show
that you appreciate the help. Most children like to please
their parents, so try to show your pleasure when your child
helps.

The most important feedback your child can receive is
that things are where they are expected to be. Thus, try
not to rearrange and change things at this crucial time. If
you have to change, be sure to teach your child the new
locations so that failures in finding things are minimized.
The world is new and big, and your child needs the security now of being able to predict where things can be
found.

Awareness of the Environment
18–24 Months

A STEP CHILDREN CAN TAKE
To learn that the environment
is predictable

SPECIFIC ABILITY NO. 10
They can become aware of the
duration of intervals and
the sequence of events in
their daily routines

1. What this ability means to children

As children develop the ability to remember routines,
sometimes the detail and accuracy with which they remember are almost uncanny. Many children notice if one
small part of a routine is omitted. They insist that things be

done just so, with no omissions or changes. This desire for consistency is important to children at this level of development because it gives them a sense of security. After all, their small world contains so much that is new. How wonderful to be able to count on household routine.

Children do not understand duration of intervals and sequence of events in the same way adults do because they are too immature to have an adult concept of time. However, they eventually learn about time from experiencing intervals and sequences. Some children find the concept of time very difficult even when they reach the age of twelve or thirteen years. Perhaps their difficulty stems from the lack of routine in their second year of life.

2. Parents can provide

Be sure to provide your child with routines which the family follows day by day. At times you may feel as though routine restricts your family. However, when you remember the important part routine plays in development, you will probably feel it is worthwhile. Besides, this stage doesn't last forever. Six months may be enough if your child receives the needed security, and learns that the environment of the home is predictable.

Of course, part of learning about routine is for your child to learn that routines are broken at regular intervals. When working parents have a day off, workday routines are set aside. Your child can learn to count on doing something different on those days. Holidays, church school, family visits, and traveling will occur, too. The important point is that these departures from routine have a basic day-by-day routine from which to depart.

When something different is going to happen, take the

time to explain and prepare your child. Considering your child's feelings is always worthwhile. Forget surprises at this stage. Your child needs security with no unprepared changes.

In an earlier section (see pp. 75–78) we spoke about teaching your child words having to do with sequence (after, before, later). Continue with these words and, now, add duration words: "We will take a short walk." "We will take a long walk." "I will talk on the telephone for a little while." Use the word *time* as well. "It is time to take a bath." "We have time for one more tower." "It is time to go to the store."

"It is time to" is an effective way to teach children about routines. Make a large poster for the refrigerator door or bulletin board or wherever it is convenient and readily seen. Draw a clock face in the middle and attach a single hand with a paper fastener. Around the perimeter of the clock, draw pictures of bathtime, naptime, suppertime, and whatever other activities are routine in your house. Let your child turn the hand to the activity to be done next.

Try making up little songs and rhymes. For example:

> Now it's time to eat a meal
> Eat a meal, eat a meal
> Now it's time to eat a meal
> Because it's suppertime

3. Feedback

Encourage your child to feel secure in daily routines. If your child insists upon a certain routine, respect that right for security, even though it means fifteen stuffed animals plus two books and one truck in the bed at bedtime, each article placed just so in a given order. These routines are important as your child learns that the environment is predictable.

Awareness of the Environment
18–24 Months

A STEP CHILDREN CAN TAKE
To learn that actions
have consequences

SPECIFIC ABILITY NO. 11
They can learn that their
actions may have conse-
quences related to adult
approval or disapproval

1. What this ability means to children

For children recently so egocentric, even becoming *aware* of parents' reactions to their actions is a step toward becoming socialized. Actually, children are still not concerned about their parents' feelings *except* as those feelings relate to themselves. They do learn that their actions have consequences. When parents disapprove of their behavior, the consequences are unpleasant. When parents approve, life is much more rewarding.

Feedback has been an emphasis all through this book. However, now children are at a developmental level when they begin to be aware of feedback themselves. They begin to realize more and more consciously that their actions result in feedback and have consequences. One of the most meaningful areas in which children learn about consequences has to do with their parents' approval and disapproval. After all, parents are still very, very important to their two-year-old child.

2. Parents can provide

Consistency is the most important thing you can provide. If your child is to learn about the consequences of behavior, your reactions must be consistent. Do not disapprove of a particular behavior one day, and approve of that behavior the next day. Always disapprove of that behavior; or always approve.

You can help your child learn what behaviors result in your approval and what behaviors bring your disapproval. Here are some suggestions to consider for your child:

A. Make a deck of flash cards with pictures of children behaving in an approved manner and children behaving in a disapproved manner. Have an extra card with a smiling parent's face on one side and a frowning parent's face on the other. As you show the picture cards, reverse the parent's face card appropriately. Then, let your child reverse the face card, depending on approved or disapproved behavior, as you go through the picture cards again.

B. Tell you child little stories about children, describing their actions, and their parents' reactions, and the happy or unhappy consequences.

C. Make an Approval Badge for your child to wear when behavior meets with your approval.

3. Feedback

Your approval and disapproval constitute the feedback for your child. Your hope is that your child is learning to be aware of consequences. Therefore, when your child shows evidence of thinking about the results of certain actions, praise and encourage this awareness. It is part of learning about the predictability of your child's world. The predictable consequences of actions is a lesson we all must learn, and your child can begin to learn this lesson in the important second year of life.

Although this section borders on a discussion of discipline, we have deliberately avoided discussing discipline directly because the thrust of this section is that actions have consequences. Discipline is discussed on pp. 104–106.

Awareness of the Environment
18–24 Months

A STEP CHILDREN CAN TAKE
To learn that behavior
can have a purpose

SPECIFIC ABILITY NO. 12
They can pick up their
toys and put them away

1. What this ability means to children

Children of this level of development gain satisfaction from completing an activity. "All done" is frequently heard. Many children go through a phase of extreme neatness; each object must be in its particular place down to a fraction of an inch. Routines must be followed in the minutest detail. The child's need for security accounts for all this fussiness. As children become more aware of the world around them, which is increasingly complex, the complexity is almost overwhelming. They must have security as they become accustomed to their environment.

When you understand why your child is particularly neat and orderly at this level of development, you might as well use that orderliness to good advantage. You can teach your child to put toys away, each toy in its own place. Messy stages may occur later as your child becomes older but, right now, picking up belongings *can* become a habit.

Your child's orderliness can also be a beginning in the lesson that actions can have a purpose. When children pick up their toys they can pick up for the purpose of keeping the house neat and for the purpose of helping you. As children experience the purposive behavior of picking up their belongings, they will be laying groundwork for the positive outlooks of self-confidence and independence and that their world is predictable.

2. Parents can provide

If possible, give your child a private place for putting away toys. A private place may be anything from a bookshelf to a toy chest, but it belongs to your child and no one else.

You will probably need to begin by picking up toys with your child. You can make it fun. Here are some suggestions:

A. Tell simple stories about children who help their parents by putting their toys away.
B. Sing a song like "This is the way we put toys away, toys away, toys away."
C. Place a label on the special shelf to tell the world it is just for your child's toys.
D. Put stars on a poster whenever your child picks up.
E. Set a timer that rings when it is time for your child to stop play and start picking up.
F. Make a "Happy Helper" badge.

3. Feedback

Praise and reward your child by any method that is effective when toys are picked up. Show your appreciation for the help your child gives you. Communicate your pleasure that your child is grown-up enough to complete the task of putting away belongings.

Since your child is helping you, you might reserve the time saved by spending special time together. There can be an extra story at bedtime because your child helped and saved you time. You can have a longer time together at the playground because the toys are all picked up and put away. The reward of more of your time adds a broader purpose for your child to be neat and orderly and expands the experience of purposeful behavior.

Awareness of the Environment
18–24 Months

A STEP CHILDREN CAN TAKE	SPECIFIC ABILITY NO. 13
To learn that behavior can have a purpose	They are ready for challenging play materials which require concentration

1. What this ability means to children

Child development specialists, a number of years ago, told us that a child's *attention span* increased with age and that very young children would not stick with any one activity for more than a few minutes. Many parents, however, know better. One particular child will spend hours in the sandbox making cakes and pies. Another child will work a long time putting puzzles together. Another will play house with Teddy bear all morning. Attention span and concentration are matters of matching the activity to the child's maturation and interest.

Puzzles can have several pieces now because not only circles but squares, triangles, and diamonds can be handled with success. Put-together-take-apart toys can be more complicated. Drawing will include circular strokes in addition to the straight lines of a few months ago. Towers, now, are several blocks high and many children can string beads.

At this developmental stage imagination begins to develop because children can use one object to represent something else. A child with a line of little blocks may be pretending a traffic scene; a child with a box with farm animals may be pretending to be a farmer. Children will concentrate on their pretend play.

Challenge and concentration are essential to purposeful behavior. Most children can be challenged and can concentrate on purposeful behavior before they are two years old.

2. Parents can provide

Your research of your child will be essential. Observe so that you can decide what toys will challenge your child. How good is finger dexterity? Are wrists flexible enough for drawing or shoveling? Is eye-hand coordination ready for advanced puzzles? Observe carefully, then by trial and error experiment with new toys. Avoid giving your child a toy that is too advanced because you do not want to create frustrations and failures. You want your child to have success but still be challenged enough to concentrate with a purpose.

You can also provide time. When your child is concentrating, allow uninterrupted time. Do not intrude on happy, solitary play. Of course, there will be times when your child wants to play with you. But your child will treasure those times when concentration on challenging play will exclude you.

3. Feedback

Taking pride in children's accomplishments reinforces their satisfaction with their purposeful activity. Some children like to have their drawings or buildings or completed puzzles on display for all to see.

Let your child know that you are available to help if you are needed. However, encourage your child's independent play. Some children like to be told that they are *big* or are *growing up so much* when they have accomplished a project. This does *not* work with a few children, so discover what reinforces your child. You can try stars or stickers on a chart to reinforce purposeful behavior. As children gradually realize that they can do projects for a purpose, their self-confidence and independence will increase. Purposeful behavior also contributes to children's experiencing predictability in their world.

Awareness of People
12–15 Months

A STEP CHILDREN CAN TAKE
Learning to become aware
of differences in others

SPECIFIC ABILITY NO. 1
They can enjoy social
give-and-take with adults

1. What this ability means to children

Infants in the first year of life are hardly aware of persons as separate from themselves. Children at this developmental level are aware of people and are even beginning to distinguish between people, particularly adults. The baldheaded man looks different from the woman at the check-out counter in the grocery store. Strangers may be frightening because now your child sees differences that are new.

You can help your child develop perceptions of other people by starting experiences of social give-and-take. A child who enjoys social interchange is building the confidence that is needed to be comfortable with all kinds of people. However, first experiences should be enjoyable. Begin with people who are very familiar and who will enjoy playing with your child. Also, it is best to start with adults.

Adults will play with a child in order to meet the child's needs rather than their own. When a very young child hands a toy to an adult, the adult is willing to hand it right back, because that's the way the child wants to play that game. Other children not only keep the toy but grab others that belong to the child. A grabbing game is clearly frustrating to the young child and makes for unenjoyable social give-and-take.

2. Parents can provide

Some parents overpower children by exposing them to quantities of people so that they become aware of differences. Provide your child with opportunities to see only a few people at a time. Your child may begin with a good bit of sober staring at people. Social give-and-take may come gradually. Don't force and eventually the staring stage will be replaced by some small social advance from your child.

A social game most children love is just walking with an

adult. Very often, children will want a hand held or they may only want to hold onto one finger. These small advances are very important social give-and-take at this young developmental level.

Watch for the times when your child wants to give you something. The gift may be only a pebble or the touch of the hand on your leg. However, a gift has been made which is another social advance. You should recognize that your child may want that pebble right back again. You can respond with pleasure and graciousness and return what your child has given you.

A relaxed, easygoing climate in the home, when there are visitors, is valuable for parents to provide. Avoid drawing undue attention or showing off your child. The pace of social give-and-take should be left to the child.

3. Feedback

Encourage your child when differences in people are noticed. Noticing differences is an early and necessary step along the road to associating happily with others. Reinforce your child when social give-and-take with you or others is initiated and share your joy in these social advances. Your child has much to learn to become the social person that is possible. See that these beginning steps are happy experiences.

Awareness of People
12–15 Months

A STEP CHILDREN CAN TAKE
Learning to become aware
of differences in others

SPECIFIC ABILITY NO. 2
They can examine other
babies by touch and feel

1. What this ability means to children

Children have differentiated between adults and have recognized other older children as different from adults, particularly if there are siblings in the home. But another baby is probably a new experience. At first, another baby is just another object to explore. The fact that a baby is a person, not an object, can only be learned by exploring babies: seeing them, touching them, and hearing them. Parents who do not understand this are often horrified when their child *assaults* a visitor's baby. A very young child poking, pulling hair, pinching, hitting, and/or squeezing another baby is very common. The child is trying to find out what that strange object is, that we call a baby. The baby on the receiving end will probably reciprocate and both will learn valuable lessons.

2. Parents can provide

You can provide understanding and patience. Of course, you must provide supervision. A free-for-all might become damaging. Besides, you want these first social steps to be happy ones. Therefore, put up with a little poking and hair-pulling, but be ready to separate the babies if the going gets too rough. Then show your child how to pat and stroke gently.

Some mutual understanding with the parent of the other baby wouldn't be a bad idea. It might save you a friend.

3. Feedback

While you will want to encourage exploring another baby, you will also want to encourage permissible exploration. Praise patting and stroking. Remove the child who is hurting the other baby and divert attention to some other activity. You will have to study each situation and be sensitive about your best procedure. Keep things as happy as possible as your child learns that babies are people, even though they are very different from adults and older children.

Awareness of People
12–15 Months

A STEP CHILDREN CAN TAKE
Learning to become aware
of differences in others

SPECIFIC ABILITY NO. 3
They can imitate behavior
and vocalizations of others

1. What this ability means to children

Is there a copycat in your house? Your child is eagerly observing and imitating what is seen and heard. Your mannerisms and your speech are copied. You will be amazed at what good imitators these very young children can become. They'll imitate mother on the phone, dad puffing on his pipe, the noise of the vacuum cleaner, even the way a particular woman blows her nose. They imitate and learn. Here is your opportunity to use this ability to imitate as a way for your child to differentiate between people. Children at this developmental level know that people, at least grownups, are separate from themselves and now they are learning that people are different from each other. These differences are beginning to be recognized and imitated.

2. Parents can provide

Provide your child with exposure to good models to imitate. The primary models are, of course, parents. If you have been talking baby talk, it is strongly suggested that you stop. Your child will not benefit by imitating baby talk. Observe yourself and the other adults in your home and you will discover the kinds of models your child imitates. Your observations may be rather embarrassing when you find out that an unattractive behavior is being imitated.

Your child will probably imitate you if you do no more than provide a model. However, you can use this ability of imitation for fun games with your child. One of you makes a funny face, the other imitates. Most children love this game and you can play the game with words and with fun sounds, even whistling.

Some children enjoy a mirror in which they can watch themselves practicing imitations of others. Provide a toothbrush because your child will probably love to imitate you brushing your teeth. Kleenex for nose blowing is another favorite and a toy telephone may be useful. Some children try to imitate hair brushing and combing, but don't expect very much in the grooming department at this early age. The results will be hair-rumpling more than anything else.

Together with your child act out differences in people you see; father's low voice, mother's higher voice; the way different people cough or blow their noses; the ways different people sit in chairs or walk, talk, or use their hands. Once you and your child have mastered this game, you will find all sorts of differences that can be imitated.

3. Feedback

Encourage your child to imitate. You may want to ignore a few imitations that are particularly embarrassing, but praise and enjoy the acceptable imitations. Particularly encourage imitations of behaviors or speech that differentiate between people. Noticing differences is important because it expands your child's awareness of people. People become of more and more interest and this is a step along the way to more social behavior as your child matures.

Awareness of People
12–15 Months

A STEP CHILDREN CAN TAKE
Learning to become aware
of differences in others

SPECIFIC ABILITY NO. 4
They can begin to adjust
to strangers

1. What this ability means to children

Children vary a great deal in the way they adjust to strangers. There are a few fortunate children who go through few stages of fearing strangers; they are seldom shy or timid. Perhaps your child will be like this. What is much more likely is that your child will be afraid of strangers for a month or so and then have a period of being quite open and friendly. Some children are very frightened of strangers who are particularly noisy and talk in a loud voice. Some children will approach women but not men, or vice versa. Some children need a period of solemn staring before they will approach a new person.

The reasons for these wide differences among children are related to their present perceptual maturity and their past experiences. Consider perceptual maturity. Not so long ago your child was hardly aware of differences between people. Then noticing that there were big people (adults) and little people (children) began. Now, your child is able to perceive much finer distinctions. People have different noses, eyes, mouths, hair, and so forth. The stimuli children receive as they see, hear, and touch people have greatly increased in quantity and quality. These stimuli can be quite overwhelming for some children; they need time to adjust.

Past experience plays a part, too. If children have seen no strangers in the past, the first new faces may be upsetting. If they have seen strangers before and have always had happy experiences, more strangers may not be upsetting. However, if children have had unhappy experiences in the past, their heightened perceptual awareness may cause suspicion or fear of all strangers.

2. Parents can provide

You are getting to know your child better every day. Study behavior with strangers so that you can follow your child's pace. If you force social contacts with strangers before your child is ready, you may only lose ground. Your child may need good old-fashioned cuddling from you when strangers are frightening, or maybe just holding your hand will be enough. On the other hand, you may have a socially aggressive child who will approach anyone and everyone. You will have to do your best to avoid your child's approaching someone who might dislike a young child's advances. The experience might become an unhappy experience and that is something you want to avoid.

Besides providing opportunities to see new people, there are other things you can do to help your child adjust to differences in people. Read stories about people your child is likely to encounter: the mailman, the grocery clerk, the bus driver, etc. Pictures of different people can be

shown. Every few days you can post a new picture on a
bulletin board.

3. Feedback

Encourage your child whenever an interest is shown in
other people. Praise friendly advances to others. Give your
child the security of knowing that you are near at hand to
comfort if necessary. Above all, do not force or shame if
your child is timid and withdraws from new people. Try to
divert attention until your child is ready to make advances
to a new person.

Try to protect your child from unhappy experiences
and increase happy experiences with strangers. Reinforce
your child's happy adjustments to others because it is your
positive feedback that leads to your child's developing
positive basic outlooks. You are helping your child now
with an early step in future attitudes toward people.

Awareness of People
12–15 Months

A STEP CHILDREN CAN TAKE
A growing enthusiasm to
learn about social inter-
action

SPECIFIC ABILITY NO. 5
They can play simple
games with parents

1. What this ability means to children

As children begin to recognize that people are persons
and not just objects or even extensions of themselves, they
begin to enjoy games with their parents. They are becoming aware of interchange between people. They engage in

an action, their parent responds; back and forth. The interaction is very flattering to the child who desires to be the center of attention. To an egocentric child, and all very young children are quite egocentric, getting attention is bread and butter; it is basic to their experiencing and learning. Therefore, an eagerness for social interaction can be easily nurtured in these self-centered children by the simple expedient of playing games that center around the child.

Children begin with self-interests and, as they experience successful social interactions with self at the center, they do mature in time. Their self feelings diminish in importance and they begin to appreciate the feelings of others. You will be laying the foundations for this social potential as you help your child develop an eagerness for playing simple games with you.

2. Parents can provide

Initiate some games with your child even though these games may seem silly to you. They are important to your child. Try several games to find those your child enjoys the most.

Peek-a-boo games are generally popular. Peek-a-boo can be from hands over the face, an apron or cloth over the face, or from behind the curtain.

Hide-and-seek games or "where's the baby?" are fun.

"I'm going to catch you" is fun, with the parent on all fours. Rough-housing and "bag of rags" are other games. Be a little careful about the game becoming too stimulating for your child to handle. As with all games, watch as your child tires, and stop before exhaustion threatens to result in a tearful conclusion.

3. Feedback

Your child needs the important feedback that you enjoy playing games together. Encourage and praise your child as you play together and show that it is fun for you. This kind of feedback will help your child to be eager for other social interchanges. Each successful game experience will build toward your child's happy feelings about people.

Awareness of People
12–15 Months

A STEP CHILDREN CAN TAKE
A growing enthusiasm to learn about social inter-action

SPECIFIC ABILITY NO. 6
They can enjoy an audience

1. What this ability means to children

Many children at this level of development discover that not only are others persons, but also they are persons who respond to little children. Since these egocentric children relish attention, an audience that laughs and claps is like having ice cream and candy. Some children develop quite a repertoire of tricks to perform whenever they get a chance. Some of these tricks are winking, acting coy, making funny faces, dancing, and "reading" the newspaper. You might say these tricks are showing off or being a regular ham. No matter, attention-seeking behaviors are a good device to use in developing your child's enthusiasm for social interaction.

2. Parents can provide

You may need a little tolerance to let your child have stage center. Some of the play acting may be quite silly to you. However, as you realize that showing off is building eagerness to interact with others, you can be more appreciative of your child's performances.

Some families have found that a regular time, such as after meals, is a good time for the whole family to enjoy the baby. Some children like to have an audience of only one or two, while others think the more, the better. There are children who will perform only for family, while some children will perform for anyone. Find out how your child best displays thespian tendencies. Then provide your child with appropriate opportunities.

3. Feedback

Enjoy your child's performances. Praise will encourage more performances. Help your child feel good about these interactions with others. The foundations are being built for your child's future positive attitudes about people.

Awareness of People
12–15 Months

A STEP CHILDREN CAN TAKE
A growing enthusiasm to learn about social interaction

SPECIFIC ABILITY NO. 7
They can laugh at abrupt sounds and funny faces

1. What this ability means to children

Have you thought about the beginning of a sense of humor? A child laughs spontaneously at abrupt sounds and at incongruities. The laughter is probably no more than a nervous reaction to surprise, at first. However, as the laughter is rewarded, it becomes a conditioned response and the basis for the child's sense of humor. A sense of humor is very important for a child to develop because humor is probably essential to all future social interaction.

You may have some difficulty understanding why some things are so funny. Does your child whoop uproariously at a face without eyes, at an abrupt sound, at the word "tickle"? Does your child laugh while edging closer and closer to a forbidden object? These behaviors are common evidences of a potential sense of humor in very young children.

Never mind whether or not you understand the amusement your child enjoys. Be glad that a sense of humor is developing. Laughter can add to success at social interactions and make your child eager for more interaction.

2. Parents can provide

An atmosphere of carefree good humor within your home will certainly help. You can play the clown, make funny faces and sounds, drop the rings in a juggling act or crawl around like a dog barking in order to get your child laughing. Let your child get in on the act, too. Try on an oversized hat and together look in the mirror. Your child may think that is funny. Make a recording of music that has sudden gaps of silence. Some children think this is terribly funny.

You will just have to experiment to find out what makes your child laugh. Adult, verbal jokes may be meaningless while language is still such a problem. Usually abrupt sounds and some sort of incongruity will get these very young children laughing.

3. Feedback

When your child sees humor in a situation and laughs, laugh together as reinforcement. Encourage laughter every chance you can; it's good for social interchange. Relax and enjoy your child as a sense of humor is developing.

Awareness of People
12–15 Months

A STEP CHILDREN CAN TAKE
To learn to adjust to the
wants of others

SPECIFIC ABILITY NO. 8
They can laugh at minor
bumps and bruises

1. What this ability means to children

Nobody wants to live with a "crybaby." In adjusting to the wants of others, your child can learn to take bumps and bruises in stride. You can count on numerous spills and tumbles in these first months of walking. However, children are tougher than you think and should not be encouraged to cry over the least little hurt.

We are not talking about making Spartan stoics out of little children. We are not suggesting that children be taught to suppress tears when they are really in pain. But all too often, here is what happens. The child trips and falls down. The cry may be only surprise at being tripped by the chair which got in the way. The doting parent runs to the child, cooing, "You poor baby. Does it hurt?" The parent smothers the child with sympathy and attention, excellent reinforcers for hurting and crying at the next tumble. Children will do what brings them the most attention.

You can change that pattern with your child. Instead of reinforcing tears and crying, you can reinforce laughing at minor bumps and bruises.

2. Parents can provide

Reserve attention and sympathy for only big hurts. You will have to observe your child carefully so that you can distinguish when the comforting is needed. However, when minor mishaps occur, provide diversions so that the hurt does not receive attention. Say "oops" and laugh (with, not at your child), blow away the hurt and introduce a new activity. With some falls, your child may get right up again without needing any attention from you. Don't impose unneeded attention. Your sensitive handling of bumps and bruises can contribute to your child's gradually adjusting to getting along with others by not being a crybaby.

3. Feedback

We have been talking about feedback in the last paragraph. You can go a bit further and add praise when your child is able to laugh off a little hurt. Be sure your child receives attention for laughing. Gradually, as your child gets older, you will have to explain first-aid rules. Certainly you are not trying to get your child to laugh at a bleeding cut without receiving first aid. However, you are avoiding making your child a crybaby about minor discomforts; good groundwork for future, successful adjustment socially.

Awareness of People
12–15 Months

A STEP CHILDREN CAN TAKE
To learn to adjust to the
wants of others

SPECIFIC ABILITY NO. 9
They can learn that they
are allowed to touch some
things but not others

1. What this ability means to children

As children learn to walk, run, and climb they can reach more and more objects. They are exploring, experimenting with their five senses, because this is the way they learn. As their awareness matures, they perceive new possibilities every day. Think how exciting it must be to have a brand-new, fresh world differentiating before your eyes.

In this book parents are urged to encourage their child's explorations. However, a limit is reached, because of safety factors. You do not want your child to get hurt, nor do you want your prized possessions damaged. You, of course, must set the rules and, once you do, stick with the rules.

Consistency is the key word. "No no," and "don't touch," can be associated with being restrained or removed, if, and only if, your child actually is *consistently* restrained or removed. Sometimes just a head shake or gesture or frown on your part will be enough, but it must be consistent. Your child, in learning what is forbidden, may be the kind of child who tests the rules frequently to see if they still apply. Such children may approach a forbidden object, glance at their parents, and still proceed to touch, keeping close track of parental reaction. They are asserting their newfound independence. Children must be restrained or removed so that they continue to associate an order not to touch with the forbidden object. If you can just force your-self to be consistent in the feedback your child receives, eventually you will be obeyed. Children really prefer the most pleasant feedback they can get. Frowns and "no no's" are not very pleasant.

2. Parents can provide

Provide plenty of objects your child is allowed to touch, and praise and encourage touching and exploring these objects. Keep the number of *untouchables* to a minimum. You cannot get rid of the stove or the gate at the head of the stairs or locks on doors. But, do you really need that china vase on the end table or the tippy lamp on the desk? Of course, you will lock up medicines and dangerous cleaning fluids. In other words, study your child's environment. Make it as safe as possible. Decide what your child can touch and what your child cannot touch. Make what is allowed as attractive as possible. Keep what is not allowed to a minimum.

3. Feedback

"No no's" need not be harsh. The trick is to divert your child's attention away from a forbidden object to some-thing more attractive. An example may demonstrate the technique, if you don't already know the method. Your child reaches for the paring knife on the kitchen counter. You say "no no" and separate knife from child. Immediately, you hand your child a favorite stuffed animal and show how to make it dance. Your child will quickly forget the knife and you can reinforce the acceptable behavior of laughing at the silly dancing animal.

Certainly, there will be times when you encounter tears, even tantrums, as you restrain your child. However, just the mere act of lifting your child bodily starts a calming process in most children. Then you divert attention further by an attractive substitute.

Your patience and consistency will pay off in the long run, and you will be helping your child adjust to the wants of others. The others in this case are parents, but it is a beginning step toward associating happily with people generally.

Awareness of People
12–15 Months

A STEP CHILDREN CAN TAKE
To learn to adjust to the
wants of others

SPECIFIC ABILITY NO. 10
They can learn to do what
they do not want to do

1. What this ability means to children

Very young children "want what they want, when they want it." In other words, they do not like to wait. Their desires are all-important to them. This egocentrism has been mentioned often in this book. As infants, children were completely locked in self; there was nothing else. However, gradually they become aware that yes, indeed, there is something else besides themselves. There are toys, there's their house and, most importantly, there are people. They are still too immature to be aware of the fact that those people have wants of their own. The child's wants are still all-important. However, these very young children can take a step in adjusting to others' wants by learning to do what they do not want to do.

What are some of the things children dislike doing? Here is a list of common dislikes:

Having to stop an outdoor activity to come in for a meal
Being required to take a bath
Having climbing interrupted
Diaper-changing
Being dressed
Being kept inside when sick
Having to return a toy that belongs to someone else
Going to the doctor
Having hair shampooed

You have probably identified some of your child's dislikes. You may have experienced tears or tantrums as a result of requiring your child to do something disliked.

There is something happening to your child at this level of development which will help you. As children's perceptions mature and they become more and more aware of people, they begin to pay attention to consequences or the feedback from their actions. Children will do what brings the most pleasureable consequences—pleasureable to them, of course. They can even learn to do what they do not want to do, if the results bring them pleasure.

2. Parents can provide

Eventually you will want your child to respond sympathetically to your likes and dislikes. While maturation is occurring to make sympathy possible, do provide an environment where your child's wants are respected. Recognize likes and dislikes. If interruptions are bothersome, avoid swooping down and forcing an interruption. Give a few minutes for your child to adjust to stopping an activity.

In other words, replace "come to the table this instant" with "supper will be ready in five minutes, so finish up what you are doing" or "I'll set the timer so you can hear when to come to the table." Think of the amount of consideration you give adult guests who are engaged in conversation when you are ready to serve a special dinner. Your child's feelings deserve your consideration, too.

If dressing is particularly disliked, try considering your child's feelings and cooperate as far as possible. Why is being dressed disliked? If it is because your child wants to play and hates being restricted, a small toy for diversion while you proceed with the dressing may help.

Many children dislike visiting the doctor. It is probably because they fear the unfamiliar. Respect your child's wants enough to prepare for the visit ahead of time. Play doctor together so your child will know what to expect. Let a favorite toy visit the doctor, too.

Whenever your child must do something disliked, consider your child's feelings and make the disliked action as pleasant as possible.

3. Feedback

Whenever your child accomplishes something disliked, provide some kind of reward. The consequences must be pleasant as this difficult lesson of doing what is disliked is learned. You will have to decide what rewards your child. Your spoken word, "good for you," may be sufficient. "I come to the table" badge is another idea. Candy at the end of the doctor's visit, or a check mark on a getting dressed chart may be rewarding. Just be sure that your child experiences a pleasant consequence when doing what your child does not want to do. The necessity of rules for people to get along together is too abstract to be understood. However, your child can understand the experiencing of pleasureable consequences, and this is a step on the path to adjusting to other people.

Awareness of People
15–18 Months

A STEP CHILDREN CAN TAKE
To learn to take an interest
in other children's behavior

SPECIFIC ABILITY NO. 11
They can become interested
in watching other children

1. What this ability means to children

Children at this developmental level are beginning to realize that other children, and even babies, are distinct people. They may not be ready to interact with another child yet. If they do, the action will still probably be quite a bit of the poking, pinching, hair-pulling variety mentioned on pp. 91–93. However, one thing children can do, and most of them do engage in this activity, is just watch. They now listen very carefully; they are not threatened; they are experiencing what other children do and are. Many children seem to need this stage before they start actively interacting with other children.

2. Parents can provide

Give your child opportunities to watch and listen to other children. Many children like just one other child to watch at first. Some children can watch two or three at a time. Take your child to the park or playground, sit on a bench together and provide time to watch in safety. If you force your child to play with another child you may be interfering with progress. Very few children this age actually play cooperatively with another child. Be patient and let your child set the pace. Eventually, your child will be ready to do more than just watch.

3. Feedback

Encourage your child to take an interest in other children. Show that you are interested in other children but that you respect your child's need to just watch. Enjoy watching with your child.

Awareness of People
15–18 Months

A STEP CHILDREN CAN TAKE
To learn to take an interest
in other children's behavior

SPECIFIC ABILITY NO. 12
They can play next to another
child in "parallel play"

1. What this ability means to children

Parents may be surprised by this stage in social development. However, it is very common, and usually lasts for months. Children play next to each other, each doing their own thing and seemingly not even noticing each other. The stage is called "parallel play" in child-development books. Actually, the children are aware of each other, but they can enjoy the experience of being together without the threat of having to interact until they have gained more experience.

2. Parents can provide

Respect your child's need for "parallel play." You might as well abandon the idea that children will play "ring-around-a-rosy" or "follow the leader" together at this age. Your child may play games like that with you. However, your child has recognized you for some time now and feels secure with you. Differentiating between other little children is relatively new for your child. Thus, give time and opportunity for plenty of "parallel play."

Do you have a friend with a child the age of your child? Set up visits so that both children can be together under at least one parent's supervision. If the children have been together before, they may start "parallel play" at once. Otherwise, some watching from a distance may be necessary before your child is ready to play near the other child. Let the children set their own pace.

If you have a situation where the visiting child is too aggressive, snatches your child's toys, punches and kicks, it is probably best to remove your child. You do not want to over-protect, of course, or make a sissy of your child, but it is important that these very early social contacts be happy ones. Your little child needs nonthreatening, pleasant experiences of playing next to another child. Unhappy experiences may cause your child to withdraw and lose interest in other children.

Your child may enjoy picture books and simple stories about children who play beside each other. However, pay attention so that you do not move ahead of the developmental level of your child. Avoid introducing the social graces of taking turns, sharing, and playing together. At this developmental level you are only trying to give your child experiences of the pleasure of parallel play.

3. Feedback

Encourage your child to continue parallel playing. Show that you approve and are pleased by whatever interest your child takes in other children. You might place a friend's name and picture on the bulletin board to remind your child of a happy time.

Final reminders:

A. Let your child set the pace.
B. Supervise so that these very early social experiences are happy.
C. Reinforce your child's taking an interest in other children.

Awareness of People
15–18 Months

A STEP CHILDREN CAN TAKE
To learn to take an interest
in other children's behavior

SPECIFIC ABILITY NO. 13
They can imitate other
children

1. What this ability means to children

Your child has been imitating you for some time now. As interest in adults broadens to an interest in other children, your child will begin to imitate other children. Imitating may be an extension of just watching (see pp. 109–110) or an extension of "parallel play" (see pp. 110–112) or both. The imitation by your child of another child manipulating a toy, making a facial expression, coughing, or laughing can be quite comical. While you enjoy the imitations, remember their importance. Your child has a great deal to learn socially and progress is being made in learning about other children.

2. Parents can provide

Provide the same opportunities mentioned in the previous two sections. If you have not read those sections, it might be a good idea for you to read them now, because this specific ability relates to those two abilities in the early stages of social development.

Children imitate other children when they are with them. They also imitate what they have seen when the imitated child is no longer present. If you have been observant you will know whom your child is imitating. If you have not been observant you may miss the fact that an imitation is being performed; you will miss the fun.

Your child will probably imitate other children without your prompting. However, you can encourage imitating by some games with your child.

Here is one you can try. You imitate someone and ask your child to guess who it is. It is probably best for you to stick to adults. A mother's imitation of Dad smoking a pipe is apt to bring gales of laughter. A father can imitate Mom throwing a ball. Give your child a turn. Ask your child to imitate another child, and you guess who it is.

You can role-play a recent visit from a parent and child. You play the parent and ask your child to be the youngster. Play through some of the activities of the visit.

3. Feedback

Give praise when your child imitates another child and encourage further imitating. Imitating helps in learning about other children, and also sustains your child's interest in other children. Taking an interest in other children is an early step toward a happy social future.

Awareness of People
15–18 Months

A STEP CHILDREN CAN TAKE
To learn that it is fun meeting new people

SPECIFIC ABILITY NO. 14
They can make progress in adjusting to strangers

1. What this ability means to children

As children learn more and more about people and can distinguish more and more differences between people, they may be timid about meeting strangers. A few children will run right up to any and all strangers, with open friendliness. However, most children seem to need a period of watching the new person for a while, and then they will approach, touch, hold a hand, or ask to be picked up. Some children avoid men and are friendly to women. Others avoid women, but run to men. Observe your own child so that you will learn what to expect.

2. Parents can provide

If your child is going through a shy period, don't lose patience. Most children, during their second year, go through at least two of these periods. The shyness will pass in time, and you can help most by providing the needed security and understanding.

Provide opportunities for your child to see new people.

Start a "new people" list to which you add names of people you and your child meet. When you get home from a visit to the doctor, add the new nurse's name with your child. Whenever you meet new people at the store, the library, church, the playground, etc., add names to the list with your child. The list will help *you* remember names, of course, but you are showing your child that it is fun to meet new people.

3. Feedback

As far as possible, make your child's social experiences happy. As happy experiences accumulate, your child learns "it is fun meeting new people."

You will be setting a good example if you are open and friendly when meeting new people. When your child is open and friendly, give praise. These early social experiences are very important to your child's future attitudes about people.

Awareness of People
18–24 Months

A STEP CHILDREN CAN TAKE
A growing eagerness to learn more about other people

SPECIFIC ABILITY NO. 15
They can play with another child, particularly an older child

1. What this ability means to children

Most children at this level of awareness take an active interest in other children. Many seem to prefer other children to adults. Most children are now ready to interact with other children. An older child is a good first playmate because older children meet the younger child's needs and do not require that their needs be met. Children the age of your child probably will not return toys. Since *possession* is a new concept not yet mastered, little children are hoarders. Two hoarders may have difficulty playing peacefully together. An older child, on the other hand, who is past the hoarding stage, will make a good playmate for your child.

Much of playing is still the "parallel play" variety (see pp. 110-112). There is a great deal of imitation; also, make-believe play is beginning. What a thrilling time! Whereas, play used to be confined to games with adults, now, play broadens to other children. The importance of play cannot be overemphasized. Play is the way your child will learn about other children, about sharing and taking turns, about cooperating, about making others happy. The process will be gradual, to be sure. Your child must learn about possessions (see pp. 120-122) before you can expect sharing. Lessons in cooperating (see pp. 120-124) need to be learned. Your child will need to be happy before wanting to make others happy. However, your child's eagerness to know more about other children is a step in the right direction.

2. Parents can provide

Give your child opportunities to be with other children, and see that these experiences are happy experiences. That is a tall order, to be sure, but happy experiences with other children will pay important dividends for your child's future.

Can you make arrangements with other parents so that your child will have a playmate? One playmate at a time is probably best in the beginning. You will have to observe and judge your child's readiness for playmates.

A good idea is to keep a selection of toys on hand for visiting children so that your child will not have to share until ready to share. Sharing will come in time and, although you can force your child to share, you will probably be promoting unhappy associations with other children.

Some children benefit by being prepared ahead of time for a visit from a friend. Talk about the friend who is coming. Act out with your child how to meet the friend at the door, how to give the child a cookie, how to take out the toys reserved for visitors.

Read or make up stories about children playing together. Contrast happy ways to play with unhappy ways to play. You might want to post happy playtime pictures around the house. Try hanging a "happy bird" mobile where your child plays, and tell stories about the happy bird watching happy children playing and not liking to see children who hit and kick.

3. Feedback

Give praise when your child plays with other children. Praise your child, particularly, for happy playing with friends. Show your interest in the friends and how happy you are when your child has fun playing with other children.

You may want to paste "happy bird" cut-outs on a chart whenever your child has a happy social experience. You may want to encourage your child's telling the family at the supper table about happy playtimes. Your research will tell you what reinforces your child to continue building eagerness to know more about other children.

Awareness of People
18–24 Months

A STEP CHILDREN CAN TAKE
A growing eagerness to learn more about other people

SPECIFIC ABILITY NO. 16
They continue to learn how to adjust to strangers

1. What this ability means to children

If your child has had happy experiences meeting new people in the past, you may have smooth sailing. On the other hand, a great many children experience another shy stage toward the end of the second year. Their heightened awareness of people and additional discriminations, which they can now perceive, are the reasons.

Verbal ability has also increased and it is very common to hear "Who's that?" every time your child sees a new face. Your child can understand more of what you say about people and will probably be eager to learn.

2. Parents can provide

You can explain more and more to your child because of increased verbal ability. Answer questions to the extent that your child can understand. Be sensitive to the level of understanding and do not swamp your child with useless information. For example, "That is the meter reader" is useless if your child doesn't know anything about meters. Explain "He works for the people who make the lights go on when you push the switch." However, do not rely only on explanations because experiencing is still very important to your child.

As your child gets older, go to new places where seeing new strangers will be experienced. Is there a zoo near you, or a museum? Give your child plenty of time to look at people never seen before. A relaxed, unhurried pace is best for both of you.

Some training in social skills is in order if you have not already begun. It is important for your child to know certain expected behaviors, such as saying "Thank you," "Hello," "Goodbye," "How are you," "I had a nice time," and, of course, "Please." These are Golden Words. Gold stars on a chart encourage some children to use Golden Words.

You can teach your child the skills of answering the telephone. Answering the doorbell will also be important. Your child will need to learn skills for being a guest and being a host. All of these skills can be taught by role-playing. Demonstrate the skills yourself, then let your child act them out. Preparation ahead of time is important so that you can correct your child in private. Avoid correcting your child in public. As simple social skills are mastered, your child will be more secure about meeting strangers.

3. Feedback

Encourage your child's eagerness to learn about people who are new. Enjoy new acquaintances together. Praise your child as social skills are learned and used when meeting new people. When shy periods occur, respect and reassure your child. Do not force the pace with newcomers.

Your aim is for happy associations with others. If you force your child, you risk unhappy associations.

Awareness of People
18–24 Months

A STEP CHILDREN CAN TAKE
To learn to cooperate
with others

SPECIFIC ABILITY NO. 17
They can learn what is theirs
and what belongs to others

1. What this ability means to children

Learning about possessions is an early step toward learning to cooperate with others. Children this age do not really cooperate in the sense adults think of as cooperation. They still have not matured enough to have much appreciation of the feelings of those with whom they cooperate. They are still too bound up with their own feelings. However, as they develop good feelings about themselves, they begin to be aware of the feelings of others. In preparation, they can learn what belongs to themselves and what belongs to others.

Little children hoard, and this is quite normal. They want everything in sight. "It's mine" is a common expression, even though an object is not theirs. Possessing things, everything they can lay their hands on, is satisfying. You can help your child past this hoarding stage.

2. Parents can provide

Provide respect and understanding as your child learns about possessions. As children learn that certain things really do belong solely to them, they will be able to understand that certain things also belong solely to somebody else. Begin teaching what belongs to your child. Children need their own toys and their own place to keep their toys. They should not be forced to share their toys when they are just learning about their own possessions. They need time to experience the new awareness of what belongs to them.

The next lesson is what belongs to parents. Beginning with adult possessions is better than beginning with other children's possessions, because adults are not in competition for the child's possessions. Try the pointing game. "That pipe is Dad's, that pair of shoes is Mom's, whose book is that?" You might make a set of flash cards with pictures of possessions: yours, your child's, other members of the family, and play games with the cards together. Gradually, include possessions of other children. And, finally, possessions that belong to a group can be dealt with: the toys at church school, the family car, furniture, housecleaning equipment, books and records from the library.

Along with learning about possessions, your child can learn about caring for possessions. We discussed picking up toys and putting them away on pages 110–112. This is part of caring for possessions. But children can also learn to care for their clothing and the clothing of others. They can help sort, fold, and put away the family laundry. They can take charge of the clothes hamper tasks. They can take care of a pet's dish and help you in housecleaning chores. Letting your child help you take care of possessions is good training. Extra amounts of your time may be required at first, but eventually you will have quite a helper around the house.

3. Feedback

Respect your child's possessions and give praise as your possessions and the possessions of others are respected. Show your child your appreciation for whatever help is given in caring for possessions. You will have to figure out what best rewards your child. Your pleasure may be enough, or "good for you" may work. Stars on a chart can be tried. In whatever way you encourage progress, you are helping your child take a step toward cooperating with the family and others.

Awareness of People
18–24 Months

A STEP CHILDREN CAN TAKE
To learn to cooperate
with others

SPECIFIC ABILITY NO. 18
They can learn to wait
for what they want

1. What this ability means to children

Delayed gratification is another step toward cooperating with others. Little children want what they want when they want it. They drag a poor adult by one finger and point to the cookie jar on top of the refrigerator. They want that cookie immediately. But demanding children do not take into consideration the adult's other responsibilities. In order to cooperate, the child will have to wait, and children at this level of maturity can learn to wait. They can wait now because they know and trust routine and are aware of sequence of events. They can understand "wait 'til after your nap." Children at this developmental level are also aware of parent's approval and disapproval. For example, previously when they wanted something, it made no difference if the parent was on the telephone. Now, there is a difference because children are aware that their parent disapproves of interruptions while phoning.

Children at this level of development can be left with a baby sitter or at a nursery class because they can wait. With their expanding knowledge of intervals and sequence of events, they know that their parent will return for them. They may prefer to stay with their parent. However, they can now wait, and, in this sense, they cooperate.

2. Parents can provide

Consider your child in order to determine how much waiting is realistic. Your child will not wake up one morning totally able to be left by you or able to wait long periods of time for demands to be met; this will occur gradually. Begin with short periods of waiting. Observe results and be patient and understanding of your child's needs.

The first time you leave your child in someone else's care, be sure the surroundings and the baby sitter are familiar. Prepare your child ahead of time that you must leave for a little while, but that you will return. Many children like to have some of their favorite toys with them.

In preparing your child for intervals without you, try stories about children who play happily while waiting for their parents. If gimmicks work with your child, make a badge of a "Think and Think" clown who tells children what they can do while they wait. Pin it on your child's shirt as a reminder to think of what to play next.

Review pages 106–109 about teaching time intervals and continue with those activities. If the "It is Time" clock idea is no longer useful, try making a poster with a Happy

Clock Shelf drawn on it. Then every time your child waits for a demand to be met, paste a Happy Clock on the shelf.

3. Feedback

Remind your child that waiting is cooperating. Give praise when your child does wait. Show your appreciation for the cooperation. Your child will not understand much about the concept of cooperation, but the experience of pleasure that results from cooperating will be understood. A good beginning will be made to your child's associating happily with people.

Awareness of People
18–24 Months

A STEP CHILDREN CAN TAKE
Learning about being
concerned for others

SPECIFIC ABILITY NO. 19
They can treat a doll
like a baby

1. What this ability means to children

Generally, children in their second year of life are not concerned about others; they are concerned about themselves. Egocentrism is only natural, and everyone goes through this stage as a baby. This egocentrism gradually diminishes but you can expect large portions of self-centeredness for years. This section and the following two sections will tell you what you can do to help your child move toward the socially oriented human being which is possible for a child to become.

Dolls and stuffed animals are favorite toys of many children. You can encourage your child to play with these toys in a concerned manner. Then, you can reinforce behaviors which demonstrate concern. The fact that children love to imitate is a factor you have to your advantage.

2. Parents can provide

Provide your child a model to imitate. If you have a new baby in your family, the situation is ready-made. Encourage your child to imitate with a doll whatever you do with the baby. If you do not have a new baby, arrange visits to friends where your child can see little babies and how their parents care for them. Read stories and show pictures about caring for babies.

Provide dolls and doll equipment. Most children soon learn the baby-care routine and go through the routine in minute detail. They put their "baby" to bed and cover their doll with a blanket. They read stories to their doll. They get their doll up in the morning, go through a toileting routine, dress their doll, and take their "baby" out for fresh air in the baby carriage. Their pretend play with their doll is very real to little children.

Keep track of how your child is behaving with a doll. Play dolls together often so that you can be sure it is caring behaviors your child is practicing.

3. Feedback

Be sure that when your child engages in caring behaviors with a doll, the feedback received from you is reinforcing. Praise gentleness, carefulness, protectiveness, and thoughtfulness with the doll. Show your child that you approve and take joy in these behaviors.

Awareness of People
18–24 Months

A STEP CHILDREN CAN TAKE
Learning about being
concerned for others

SPECIFIC ABILITY NO. 20
They can take part in the
preparations for a new baby

1. What this ability means to children

Children are sensitive to changes in the family atmosphere. When preparations for a new baby begin, parents have an opportunity to be reassuring by giving their child new stature. Children can learn that they are an important family member preparing for the arrival of a new baby. Although they are not yet mature enough to have any emphatic concern for a new baby, children can take part in preparations. Just the physical actions are a step in the right direction. Moreover, the feeling of importance prepares the children for discovering that they must share their parents' time and attention with a new member of the family. This discovery need not lead to consuming jealousy and rivalry, as it so often does. Parents can help by preparing their older child before the new baby arrives.

2. Parents can provide

Give your child opportunities to see new babies that belong to friends or relatives. Teach your child how to pat gently, stroke, let the baby clench a finger. Most children delight in babies. Now that they are aware that babies are also people, experiencing a person smaller than themselves for a change must be quite satisfying.

A mother's pregnancy is no hidden matter. However, a

child may miss the significance of the mother's gradual change in shape. Explain to your child about the new baby, where it is, and let your child feel the baby moving. After all, the baby belongs to your child, too.

Lots of stories and pictures of babies are helpful. The tempo of doll play can increase. Show your child with a doll what you will be doing with the new baby. Let your child learn the bathing routine, the diapering and dressing routines, the nursing and burping routines. Your child will probably enjoy imitating what you demonstrate.

Be sure to include your child as you prepare the bassinette, as you prepare diapers, clothing, blankets, and bath equipment. Whenever you can, let your child help, even though you may have to spend a bit more time. Your child can fold clothes, pile diapers, smooth blankets, tuck in sheets, fetch things, move things. Provide every opportunity that you can in the preparations so that your child can feel important.

3. Feedback

Keep stressing to your child that the baby will belong to the whole family, not just to the parents. Keep stressing your child's importance in preparing for the baby and in helping to take care of the baby once it is born. An atmosphere in the home of pleasureable anticipation will help prepare your child to look forward to the new baby, and to feel a part of the whole procedure.

Encourage doll play. Praise your child's gentleness with a doll. Reinforce all behaviors that indicate concern.

Finally, before going to the hospital, explain what will be happening to you, and the baby. Explain what provisions have been made for your child at home. Preparing your child will make a big difference when you bring the new baby home. An early lesson in becoming concerned for others will have been learned.

Awareness of People
18–24 Months

A STEP CHILDREN CAN TAKE
Learning about being concerned for others

SPECIFIC ABILITY NO. 21
They can comfort and protect those who are younger, or those who are hurt

1. What this ability means to children

Children in the last months of their second year begin to feel and show affection for others. The more generalized emotions of a younger child are becoming differentiated. Now, a distinct emotion of affection for specific people begins with behaviors adults associate with affection. Children will pat their mother, cuddle their stuffed animal, hug their baby brother, or kiss their father. The ability to comfort and protect is part of this affectionate behavior.

Children will often offer toys to a crying child. A parent's tears while reading a sad story will elicit pats and kisses. The baby crying in the crib will receive strokes, or the child will run for adult aid to comfort the baby. A crying sibling receiving adult correction will be comforted by a child at this developmental level. The comforting is not true concern for others. The comforting is more self-comforting as the child associates another's hurts as self hurts. However, the comforting and protecting behaviors can be reinforced; another step in developing a later, real concern for other people.

2. Parents can provide

You are a model for your child to imitate. Therefore, if you demonstrate sympathetic behaviors to those who are younger and those who are hurt, your child will copy you. The opportunities for your child to practice comforting and protecting behaviors will probably occur in the hurly-burly of everyday life, particularly if there are other children around. Encourage your child to play a part in comforting and protecting without your monopolizing the situations.

A new baby in the home provides a wonderful opportunity for your child to practice comforting and protecting. Encourage these behaviors, but teach your child when your assistance should be requested.

A pet provides opportunities for your child to comfort and protect. You must guide your child to appropriate comforting and protecting behaviors. Little children are apt to squeeze and hug excessively and need to learn gentleness.

You have probably developed the technique of using stories, pictures, role-playing, gimmicks, posters, or whatever else "works" to motivate your child to try new behaviors and practice new skills.

3. Feedback

You probably are a master, now, in reinforcing desired behaviors. Reinforce gentleness with babies or pets, and praise your child when comforting and protecting others. Showing concern for others is an important part of associating happily with other people.

Chapter 4

FACING THE FUTURE

If you have observed your child, have tried activities, evaluated their results, revised if necessary, and continued the cycle, you have become a researcher. Your child is probably experiencing the five basic outlooks. With this kind of background the future may be faced with confidence.

Now that you are trained in researching your child, you will, no doubt, want to continue because there is much progress to be made. The egocentrism mentioned so often in this book will be with you for several more years. However, egocentrism decreases as your child learns to be empathic, to identify with others. The egocentrism probably will never disappear; we all have traces of self-centeredness. However, the mentally healthy are probably far more emphatic than egocentric.

You will want to continue learning about children in general so that you will know what to expect next for your child. Therefore, an annotated bibliography concludes this chapter. The list of books will tell you where you can read about preschool children.

You have learned that new maturational levels and new abilities are opportunities for your child to strengthen basic outlooks. You have learned how to use opportunities of expanding awareness and to provide your child with an environment calculated to stimulate and challenge either practicing a new skill or trying a new behavior. You have learned how to play games, tell stories, role-play, make posters, or whatever it is that stimulates and challenges your particular child. Finally, you know how to provide the appropriate feedback to reinforce your child toward a basic outlook.

However, you could not have accomplished all this without researching your child. Deliberate attitude education, the kind that is taught rather than caught, requires the research approach in order to be effective. Hopefully, you have mastered this rational, yet loving, approach.

As you continue to work with your child in strengthening the five basic outlooks, do not be surprised if your child is accelerated compared to other children. The books you read may say that children do not play together cooperatively until between three and four years of age. Your child may be ready for cooperative play by two and a half years because of the careful foundations you have laid in the important second year of life. On the other hand, each child is unique and your unique child may fall behind other children the same age. More foundation building may be required than is needed for other children. Determine your child's developmental level and work there. Keep as your ultimate goals those five basic outlooks, and your child will gradually develop:

A joy for learning
Self-confidence and independence
A positive self-image
The ability to associate with others happily
Trust and faith that the environment is predictable

ANNOTATED BIBLIOGRAPHY

These first books have been written specifically for parents and laymen:

Arnold, Arnold. *Teaching Your Child to Learn: From Birth to School Age.* Englewood Cliffs, New Jersey: Prentice-Hall, 1971.
> Arnold is the author of a widely syndicated newspaper column, "Parents and Children." The book is especially good in ideas for toys and games.

Brazelton, T. Berry. *Toddlers and Parents: A Declaration of Independence.* New York, New York: Delacorte Press, 1974.
> This well-known pediatrician writes to parents of children in the "terrible twos." His compassion extends to both children and their parents.

Bricklin, Barry, and Patricia Bricklin. *Strong Family, Strong Child: The Art of Working Together to Develop a Healthy Child.* New York, New York: Delacorte Press, 1970.
> The authors are child psychologists particularly interested in communication between family members.

Chess, Stella, Alexander Thomas, and Herbert G. Birch. *Your Child is a Person: A Psychological Approach to Parenthood Without Guilt.* New York, New York: Parallax Publishing Co., Inc., 1965.
> These child psychologists have been engaged in longitudinal research. They have identified types of children. This is a helpful book, particularly if your child is the "difficult" type.

Gardner, George E. *The Emerging Personality: Infancy Through Adolescence.* New York, New York: Delacorte Press, 1970.
> The author is a child psychiatrist who writes to parents and professionals. He emphasizes developmental tasks.

Gesell, Arnold, and Frances L. Ilg. *Infant and Child in the Culture of Today: The Guidance and Development in Home and Nursery.* New York, New York: Harper and Brothers, 1943.
> This is an old book, but nonetheless valuable. Children's typical behavior is described year by year.

Gordon, Ira, Barry Guinagh, and Emile Jester. *Child Learning Through Child Play.* New York, New York: St. Martin's Press, 1972.

The senior author is director of the Institute for the Development of Human Resources at the University of Florida. This is an attractive, easy-to-read book of games to play.

McIntire, Roger W. *For Love of Children: Behavioral Psychology for Parents.* Del Mar, California: Communications/ Research/ Machines, Inc., 1970.

The author is a psychologist and professor who writes for parents of all age children. He focuses on specific behaviors and gives constructive suggestions.

Pulaski, Mary Ann Spencer. *Understanding Piaget: An Introduction to Children's Cognitive Development.* New York, New York: Harper and Row, Publishers, 1971.

Dr. Pulaski, a psychologist, has written this book for parents and teachers. It is an excellent introduction to Piaget for the beginner.

Spock, Benjamin. *Raising Children in a Difficult Time.* New York, New York: W. W. Norton & Co., 1974.

Spock's book deals with children of all ages. There is one whole section on attitudes.

White, Burton L., and Jean C. Watts. *Experience and Environment.* Englewood Cliffs, New Jersey: Prentice-Hall, 1973.

This book is a report of research undertaken at Harvard. The research focuses on the interactions between mother and child and the relation of these interactions to children's competencies.

U.S. Department of Health, Education, and Welfare, Office of Child Development. *Your Child From One to Six.* Washington, D.C.: U.S. Government Printing Office, 1962.

The following books are college texts for students of child psychology. Some parents may wish to study at this level. All the authors are educators specializing in child psychology. Each text discusses motor development, development of intelligence, emotional development and social development, the influence of parents and family and the influence of other environmental factors.

Cratty, Bryant J. *Perceptual and Motor Development in Infants and Children.* New York, New York: Macmillan Company, 1970.

Dinkmeyer, Don C. *Child Development: The Emerging Self.* Englewood Cliffs, New Jersey: Prentice-Hall, 1965.

Hurlock, Elizabeth B. *Child Development.* New York, New York: McGraw-Hill Book Co., Inc., 1964.

Jenkins, Gladys Gardner, Helen Schacter, and William W. Bauer. *These are Your Children: A Text and Guide on Child Development.* Chicago, Illinois: Scott, Foresman and Company, 1953.

Jersild, Arthur T. *Child Psychology.* Englewood Cliffs, New Jersey: Prentice-Hall, 1960.

Johnson, Donald C., and Gene R. Medinnus. *Child Psychology: Behavior and Development.* New York, New York: John Wiley and Sons, Inc., 1965, 1969.

Mussen, Paul H. *The Psychological Development of the Child.* Englewood Cliffs, New Jersey: Prentice-Hall, 1963.

While self-concept is discussed in the above texts, these last two authors focus on self-concept:

Briggs, Dorothy C. *Your Child's Self-Esteem, The Key to His Life.* New York, New York: Doubleday, 1970.

This book is written for parents. It takes a holistic, developmental approach, with self-concept the consistent backdrop.

Yamamuto, Kaoru. *The Child and His Image.* Boston, Massachusetts: Houghton Mifflin, 1972.

The author wrote this book as a college text. The theoretical developments of the child's self-concept are discussed. The technical approach may be of interest to some parents.

This short bibliography is not intended to cover all books available. Nor does the author agree with everything in each of these books. However, the list gives parents places to begin in the study of child development.

Appendix

A Story of Research

As you read this book, you may suspect that a great amount of research lies behind the printed words. Research for program development is true of all of the materials produced by the Union College Character Research Project. This project has been engaged in attitude education for over thirty years. The particular focus on babies and their parents began in 1967 when Dr. Ernest Ligon, founder of the Character Research Project,* developed a research curriculum for parents of children from birth to thirty months of age. One of the resulting programs from that original research is this book about the second year of life. Thus, the story of this book begins with the 1967 research curriculum and the hundreds of parents who belonged to what was called the Infancy Design.

The 1967 research curriculum described the development of babies, emphasized the importance of parents becoming acquainted with their baby's unique self, and suggested ways parents could help their baby develop foundations for purposiveness, values and social effectiveness. Parents were asked to keep written records of their interactions with their baby and submit these reports at specified intervals for research analysis. Thus, the reader can appreciate that a considerable amount of data about babies and their parents was accumulated.

As a result of a number of research studies, the original research curriculum was revised in 1971. A further revi-

*Research on this project was assisted by grants from the Lilly Endowment, Inc.

sion was published in 1976 and made available to the general public.[1] In the meantime, the section of the 1971 edition that dealt with birth to twelve months of a baby's life was reformatted and published for the general public in 1973.[2]

Our next plan was to create a program for parents of children in their second year of life. This book was intended to supplement the 1976 book, *Let Me Introduce My Self,* and also to act as a bridge to our projected plans for program development for the rest of the preschool years. We soon found that our intentions could not be served by simply reformatting the second year section of the Infancy Design book. In order to supplement, more detail was needed. In order to bridge toward future program development, we needed to more thoroughly introduce parents to the concept of *assessment based individualized instruction.* As parents assess their child's level of development, they can more successfully individualize whatever they choose to try in the instruction of their child. The charts in Appendix II are an aid for assessment which when used with the rest of the book are our attempt to help parents with assessment based individualized instruction for their child.

The final organization of this book was preceeded by months of information gathering on the part of the research staff. There were two general sources of information that were inspected in depth. One source, of course, was the general literature from early childhood research

[1]Ligon, Ernest M., Lucie W. Barber, and Herman J. Williams. *Let Me Introduce My Self.* Schenectady, New York: Character Research Press, 1976.
[2]Ligon, Ernest M., Lucie W. Barber, and Herman J. Williams. *If You Only Knew What Your Baby is Thinking.* Burlingame, California: Panamedia Inc., 1973. Available from Character Research Press.

on infant and child development. With few exceptions, everything in this book can be corroborated in the general literature. The exceptions, those social behaviors which the general literature reserves for later age levels, were supported in analysis of our other source of information, the rich data from the parents in the Infancy Design.

We recorded more information about children between, roughly, twelve and twenty-four months than could probably go into one book. In general, we gathered three kinds of information from our two sources:

1. Information on the development of specific abilities as children become increasingly aware of themselves, their environment and other people.
2. Information about how the development of specific abilities can be related to preattitudinal goals.
3. Information about how parents can use developing abilities to promote attitude education.

We chose fifty-four abilities from the information bank on specific abilities, because these abilities met two criteria. These abilities are prominent behaviors and are easy for parents to recognize. Furthermore, these abilities relate readily to preattitudinal goals. For example, the ability to *stand alone* can be related to the preattitudinal goal, *achievement is satisfying*. The preattitudinal goals are found on the charts under the heading of "Steps Children Can Take Toward Basic Outlooks." The emphasis should be on *steps,* small blocks which together build the foundations to what with time may be recognized as attitudes. Altogether, there are twenty-two steps on the three awareness charts. While each step is distinct from every other step, inspection reveals an obvious relationship between many of the steps.

The research procedure of Dynamic Integrative Cluster Analysis identified just which steps were related to one another. The five resulting clusters of steps, or preattitudinal goals, are, in fact, the five basic outlooks. While some of the steps relate to only one outlook, others relate to two or three of the outlooks. The charts organize specific abilities and steps so that all five basic outlooks are involved.

Analysis of the parent reports from the Infancy Design provided information about how parents can successfully reinforce developing abilities of their child in such a way as to advance a step toward one or more basic outlooks. Our research results were convincing evidence that parents can and do teach their children attitudes and that the effectiveness of such teaching depends upon the parents' loving research of their own, unique child. Thus, research was basic on our part in producing this book and is essential on your part in using this book.

CHART I. GROWING IN AWARENESS OF SELF

Age of Children in General	Specific Abilities of Children in General	Check List For Your Child	Steps Children Can Take Toward Basic Outlooks	Where to Find Suggestions
12–15 months	1. They can pull themselves to a standing position		To learn that achievement is satisfying	23
	2. They can stand alone			25
	3. They can walk		To learn that there is joy in exploring on their own	26
	4. They can climb			29
	5. They can feed themselves with their fingers		To learn that it is fun to explore new skills	32
	6. They can pick up a toy, release it, and pick it up again			34
15–18 months	7. They can drink from a cup		To begin learning to develop self-confidence	35
	8. They can take off their shoes			37
	9. They can throw a ball, although crudely			39
	10. They can stack three blocks			40

Age	Item	Goal	No.
	11. They can start, stop, and start again as they walk	To learn that it is fun to explore their independence	43
	12. They can lug, tug, push, pull, dump, and pound		44
	13. They can stoop to pick things up		46
	14. They can run, although stiffly		48
18–24 months	15. They can turn single pages of a book by themselves	To learn that independence is worthwhile	50
	16. They can take off their shoes, hat, mittens, and even unzip zippers		52
	17. They can ask to go to the toilet, either verbally or by gestures		54
	18. They can learn "I," "you," "me," & "mine."	To begin learning to recognize Selfhood	56
	19. They can refer to themselves by name		59
	20. They can distinguish between what belongs to their own person (e.g., leg, eyes, nose, hair) and to themselves as persons (e.g., hat, shoes, and shirt)		60

142

CHART II. GROWING IN AWARENESS OF ENVIRONMENT

Age of Children in General	Specific abilities of Children in General	Check List for Your Child	Steps Children Can Take Toward Basic Outlooks	Where to Find Suggestions
	1. They can make a mark on paper with a crayon		A growing enthusiasm for learning about the world in which they live	63
	2. They can stack one block on top of another			65
12–15 months	3. They can experiment by putting an object in a container and re-moving it		To learn that it is fun to experiment	67
	4. They can watch objects fall as they drop them			69
	5. They can manipulate toys in relation to other toys			70

Age	Behavior	Learning goal	Page
15–18 months	6. They can throw and go after an object	To learn the joy of using curiosity to try new combinations	72
	7. They can first empty and later on fill		74
	8. They can learn the names of events and objects that give them pleasure	To begin learning about sequence and relationships	75
18–24 months	9. They can learn where things are kept	To learn that the environment is predictable	78
	10. They can become aware of the duration of intervals and the sequence of events in their daily routines		80
	11. They can learn that their actions may have consequences related to adult approval or disapproval	To learn that actions have consequences	83
	12. They can pick up their toys and put them away	To learn that behavior can have a purpose	85
	13. They are ready for challenging play materials which require concentration		87

144

CHART III. GROWING IN AWARENESS OF PEOPLE

Age of Children in General	Specific Abilities of Children in General	Check List for Your Child	Steps Children Can Take Toward Basic Outlooks	Where to Find Suggestions
	1. They can enjoy social give-and-take with adults		Learning to become aware of differences in others	89
	2. They can examine other babies by touch and feel			91
12–15 months	3. They can imitate behavior and vocalizations of others			93
	4. They can begin to adjust to strangers			95
	5. They can play simple games with parents		A growing enthusiasm to learn about social interaction	97
	6. They can enjoy an audience			99
	7. They can laugh at abrupt sounds and funny faces			100
	8. They can laugh at minor bumps and bruises		To learn to adjust to the wants of others	102
	9. They can learn that they are allowed to touch some things but not others			104
	10. They can learn to do what they do not want to do			106

Age	#	Behavior	Goal	Page
15–18 months	11.	They can become interested in watching other children	To learn to take an interest in other children's behavior	109
	12.	They can play next to another child in "parallel play"		110
	13.	They can imitate other children		112
	14.	They can make progress in adjusting to strangers	To learn that it is fun meeting new people	114
	15.	They can play with another child, particularly an older child	A growing eagerness to learn more about other people	115
18–24 months	16.	They continue to learn how to adjust to strangers		118
	17.	They can learn what is theirs and what belongs to others	To learn to cooperate with others	120
	18.	They can learn to wait for what they want		122
	19.	They can treat a doll like a baby	Learning about being concerned for others	124
	20.	They can take part in the preparations for a new baby		126
	21.	They can comfort and protect those who are younger, or those who are hurt		128

INDEX